Crash Course in eBooks

Crash Course in eBooks

Michele McGraw and Gail Mueller Schultz

Crash Course

An Imprint of ABC-CLIO, LLC

Santa Barbara, California • Denver, Colorado

Crash Course in eBooks
Library of Congress Cataloging in Publication Control Number: 2016030068

ISBN: 978-1-61069-862-7
EISBN: 978-1-61069-863-4

20 19 18 17 16   1 2 3 4 5

This book is also available as an eBook.

Libraries Unlimited
An Imprint of ABC-CLIO, LLC

ABC-CLIO, LLC
130 Cremona Drive, P.O. Box 1911
Santa Barbara, California 93116-1911
www.abc-clio.com

This book is printed on acid-free paper ∞

Manufactured in the United States of America

CONTENTS

PREFACE

Welcome to *Crash Course in eBooks*. We know this is an exciting and rapidly changing time for libraries. Our goal in writing this book is to help you and your library get started in offering eBooks to your patrons or take steps to expand your eBook collection and service.

We know that there is no "one-size-fits-all" solution that is best for every library system. While we work for a large public library system, our goal for this book is to provide a helpful roadmap for libraries to make the best decisions regardless of the size of the community that they serve. This book presents questions, explanations, and examples. We believe that the same questions apply to systems of all sizes but the answers will vary based on the needs of the individual systems.

We also hope that this book will be useful to library systems that already offer eBooks by providing a data-based method to improve current eBook service. Many libraries with existing eBook collections want to upgrade by adding additional vendors, expanding eBook offerings to include other collections (e.g., comics) providing new ways for their patrons to access their collections, or integrating APIs into your catalog. We hope that this book will help library staff make the best decisions for their institutions, and facilitate development of the best possible eBook collections for the customers that they serve.

CHAPTER 1

Why Should You Offer eBooks?

After several false starts, eBooks are here to stay. As you start or expand your eBook collection, it is helpful to look back on some of the history of eBook technology, as well as the path libraries and readers have taken to adopt eBooks. You don't need to have an exhaustive knowledge of the history of online format changes or old eReader manufacturers to manage an eBook collection. However, having a basic understanding of how eBooks have been developed for the general consumer provides the context for the challenges libraries face in delivering eBook services to patrons. Providing eBooks to patrons is more challenging than selling eBooks to consumers. In addition, a look through the history of eBook technology highlights the fact that not only eBook services continue to be in a place of change and transition, but reader's needs and expectations are as well.

When the first eBook appeared is difficult to pinpoint with certainty. Many of the differences of opinion on this topic come from different definitions of what an eBook is, since the tools and formats people used to access early online reading options varied widely. Early versions of eBooks were often called "online books" or "electronic books." These were digitized versions of titles that could be read online or downloaded onto desktop computers. Sometimes these online books could be transferred onto other devices, but that was not always the case. The primary reading experience was on a desktop computer. The reading experience did not feature much functionality beyond the basic ability to read the text of the book. For instance, it did not include many, or at times any, of the options that readers today expect. There were seldom options to adjust font size or type, to add bookmarking, note taking, or any of the other reading features we now expect in an eBook experience. But these first online books served their purpose well. If online, the books could be shared widely via an Internet connection and updated constantly. These early formats are still being used for some types of materials, and online books helped open the door to the eBooks we see today.

The first possibility for libraries to explore eBooks was in the 1990s, when the first dedicated eReaders were introduced. The Rocket eBook and the SoftBook Reader were two of the first commercially available eReaders marketed to consumers in the late 1990s. These eReaders had much of the basic functionality that we expect in a modern eReader. They were portable, although they were much thicker and heavier than today's eReaders and similar devices. And they had the capacity to store multiple eBooks. But while today's eReaders can store thousands of eBooks, these first eReaders had a capacity of around 10 books, usually without illustrations and images (http://www.gutenbergnews .org/20110716/eBooks-1998-the-first-eBook-readers/). In addition, the content and delivery platforms for these first eBooks were not highly developed. Some publishers had content available through online bookstores, but there was not enough interesting content to grab the attention of the general consumer. At this point in time, the major U.S. publishers were not producing an eBook version all of their new releases or best sellers to be sold in online bookstores. It was not until the 2000s that the right pieces came together for the general public to start embracing eBooks. The access at that time was primarily through dedicated eReaders, but smaller devices like tablets and cellphones were available with the ability to serve as an eReader as well. In addition, improved content and access management arrived, and mainstream publishers began responding with digital content, both with new releases and by digitizing their backlist. And finally the digital protection was developed for the publishers and content creators. The digital protection makes it possible for the consumer to access and use the eBook. Perhaps more importantly to the publishers and creators, digital protection allowed publishers to limit the access to only the person who had purchased or otherwise had rights to access the eBook. We'll talk more about digital protection later in the book.

Although the file types, content, devices, and digital protection were developing, libraries needed several other pieces to be in place before eBooks could become part of their collections. Vendors needed to be willing to host the digital files for libraries. Few public libraries had, or were interested in developing, the server space and technical expertise needed to host their own eBook files. To work with the existing public library models, partners or vendors had to develop ways to mimic the check-in and check-out of a physical book, since libraries weren't able to use the retail model already in place for selling eBooks directly to consumers. And because there was a need for a method to host the files and provide the check-in and check-out mechanism, vendors or partners also needed to provide a discovery layer and reading environment for patrons. These pieces started coming together around 2008 when the necessary technologies became available from vendors, and when major U.S. publishers were willing to allow electronic versions of titles to be licensed and lent by public libraries.

Libraries, in response to the marketplace and to patrons, then began contracting with these vendors to begin offering eBooks. Then began the complicated discussions and decisions made by each publisher as to what they were willing to offer to libraries and at what terms. This will be discussed in more detail later in the book. However, libraries and publishers in general, and readers to some extent, were all seeking business and service models that maintained the status quo as they moved into the new technologies and platforms. Most libraries were looking for eBook access that aligned with what they currently had for physical materials. Libraries were looking for eBook systems that offered loan periods, had access managed with library cards, had given library staff selection tools, and all of other things that libraries and their patrons were used to working with. Publishers were looking for a business model with libraries that continued to allow them to pay authors and related costs. Readers were looking for familiar titles and a process that was easy to understand, and that aligned with the way they were used to getting physical materials. As the general eBook marketplace developed, readers began expecting that the library experience of eBooks would be as easy as obtaining an eBook from an online bookstore. New vendors came into the market, delivering services that weren't needed even a few years earlier. While there were significant pressures on all parties to change their business and use models, sometimes substantially, there was also pressure to build an eBook model that was very similar to the print model that everyone had used for decades. That tension continues to exist, and will remain part of the library, publisher, vendor, and reader dynamic for the foreseeable future.

All of these transitions are still progressing, and the landscape continues to undergo rapid shifts and changes. If your library is just getting started with eBooks, how do you enter such a fast-moving process? If your library is already providing eBooks, how do you make changes or additions to your service? These shifts and changes are daunting and can impact your library and your patrons in unexpected ways. If you implement a certain plan or strategy, you will likely need to make adjustments shortly after implementation due to shifts in reader expectations or technological changes. Your patrons may be new to eBooks, or may have been using eBooks since they were first available, many formats and devices ago. But the good news is that we are all shifting, changing, and re-implementing together.

Our hope for this book is that it provides your library with a blueprint or map to help you think through the steps you may need to consider if or when you offer eBooks to your patrons. We believe that it is always best to start with considering the needs of your patrons when considering a new service, so that is the focus of this first chapter. We'll delve into discovering what your patrons want in regards to eBooks, offering ideas and suggestions on how to connect with your patrons that you can modify to suit your situation.

Once you have an understanding of your patrons' needs and expectations, Chapter 2 will cover many of the components that need to be present to make offering eBooks to library patrons even possible. Our intent is not to go into exhaustive detail or even mention specific products or vendor names except as examples, but to simply give you an overview of the myriad number of parts that need to be in place to make offering eBooks happen for libraries.

Being aware of the parts and pieces that make up the eBook system will help you decide what path you would like to take when offering eBooks to your patrons. This is the focus of Chapter 3. We'll talk about three paths: providing access to free eBooks, creating your own system, and contracting with a vendor or vendors. Most of our focus in this book will be on vendor-based eBook systems because this remains the most common path for libraries at this time. However, many libraries and consortia are at least considering developing their own systems, so we will cover the value that they're seeing in doing so and what is involved in creating a system instead of working with a vendor.

In Chapter 4, we'll spend time talking about what it takes to implement a vendor-based product, including budgeting, selection, establishing circulation rules, technical support, staff training, and related topics. We also include sample ideas for an RFP process as well ideas for evaluating vendor products. Our hope for this chapter is that as you work through the topics and hopefully find the questions we pose helpful in clarifying your thinking, you will be able to develop an implementation plan that suits your needs.

We move back to focusing on patrons in Chapter 5 with a discussion about how to connect your patrons to your eBook collection. The discussion includes suggestions for creating a marketing and promotional strategy, offering reader's advisory in a digital world, determining what your staff can and can't do with a patron's device, and more. Some of the topics are ones we're familiar with when we think of other collections we have in our libraries. Others, like those involving patron devices and other technologies, are more unique to this topic of eBooks.

After implementation, there is usually a sigh of relief that this new product is up and running. But as we all want our new endeavors to be successful, we offer Chapter 6 as a discussion on how to figure out if you have implemented this new collection and service for your patrons correctly. We focus on three main points to consider: looking at your budget, your access points, and your services, and putting what you discover about your eBooks into the context of all of your collections and services. We hope that the discussion about success, whatever you find and however you define it, leads you ways to make any needed changes. We also hope that your success leads to messaging you can use to talk to those most important to your library system, your stakeholders.

Chapter 7 is all about evaluating your library's success and planning for further success. Once you know what's working and what's not working (Chapter 6), then you can move on to topics like expansion. We not only want to talk about how to grow, but also how to maintain and manage what you already have in place. With regards to growth, we offer a brief discussion about how to determine data to collect in order to make decisions. We also provide a framework for weeding your eBook collection. Weeding may seem like an odd topic to have in a chapter about success. Obviously, eBooks don't take up physical space on your shelves, but having the "wrong" eBooks in the way when your patrons are looking for particular topics means your collection needs to be reviewed to keep it meaningful for your patrons. Managing your collection contributes to your ongoing success.

Our last major topic of this book is how to put this whole topic of eBooks back into what's happening in the wider world. In Chapter 8, we talk about how to stay connected with topics that may affect what develops in the world of eBooks. Just as we want to continually check back in with our patrons to be sure we're offering what they want us to offer, we need to check in with what's happening with the technology that is used for eBooks. A change in technology can radically change the systems we are using. Just being aware of what's being talked about and possibly developed can make it easier for us to adapt.

We know that every library or library system is different, and the needs of our communities are unique. Because of these factors, this book is not intended to be prescriptive. Instead, we offer ideas and suggestions that you can use to determine what course of action may best fit your community, and will help you offer the best possible eBook service for your patrons.

HOW TO START

You're reading this book because you're interested in providing eBooks for your patrons. While there are as many ways to do this as there are libraries taking this step, there are ways to get started that are more effective, and that can speed up your process, helping you move more quickly from planning to getting eBooks into the hands of your readers.

Start with Your Patrons

There are many technical elements to consider when you decide to offer eBooks and it's easy to get lost in the details as you start looking at options. Before you delve into all of the technical issues and considerations, we suggest that you start by focusing on your patrons, since they're the reason your library is even considering launching this new collection. Spending the time to discover what your patrons are doing, expecting, and wanting in terms of eBooks will give you a foundation as you start exploring the more technical side of eBooks.

It may seem easiest to start by looking at vendors or platforms, or by evaluating devices or budget options. But taking a step back and considering your patrons' needs and interests will help to guide the process as you start exploring those other questions. Reconciling what your patrons want and expect with what you want to and are able to provide before considering the technical elements can bring clarity when choosing the best path forward. It is worth the time to start this as a service-first process, and not lead only with technology or collection concerns.

Discovering What Your Patrons Want

Wherever you are in your plan to add eBooks—just getting started or with an eBook collection already in place—the beginning question is the same: what do *your* patrons want? You need to ask the question with the knowledge that the answers will most likely change quickly, and that's OK. You need to start somewhere, and getting the pulse of your patrons' interests is the first step in the process.

To get started, review your own circulation data for all types of materials to determine how patrons have been using your collection. Look at circulation data as granularly as possible. Start at a high level first and then work into the details of collections. For example, rank the highest- to lowest-circulating collections by age destinations: adult, children's, easy, young adult, teen. Then take another step into the data, looking at fiction versus nonfiction. Finally, look at what is circulating within the specific parts of your library's fiction and nonfiction collections, if the data is available. When you reach this level of data, can you tell, for example, if your patrons prefer thrillers to literary fiction or vice versa? Or perhaps you can tell that your patrons are checking out biographies of musicians, but are not checking out biographies of sports figures.

While the way patrons will use an eBook collection may not always track with the way they use a physical collection, the circulation data about how they are currently using physical materials is a good way to get a snapshot of what's already happening. Taking time to look at the information you already have about what's being used will help set a course for an eBook collection and service decisions, and may also help make a large change seem a little more manageable.

Also, take advantage of other data points from patrons that would give clues as to what patrons would be interested in an eBook collection. Suggestions for books to purchase process or lists of what patrons have been requested via an interlibrary loan process are a couple of examples of other data points that can be used. Just as with circulation data, look for trends. Diving deeper into the data, are there more requests for purchases from mainstream or popular publishers, or are patrons looking for smaller or local publishers and self-published titles? Sort this into as many categories as needed, based on what's available and what will be helpful to help your library create a collection plan. While this information may align with trends in circulation data, there may be differences, since this is where patrons are communicating about what they'd like to see in the library's collection, it's not the use of the current collection. Both types of information are valuable when looking to design a new collection; what's currently being used and what patrons wish they had available in the library collection, because the two types give a more complete picture of patron needs.

This type of review is also valuable because it may highlight how patron preferences for different formats are changing. As eBook use has expanded, readers of some types of materials have moved more quickly and deeply into eBooks. For example, surveys have shown that romance readers are moving away from print materials, and many are becoming primarily eBook readers (https://www.rwa.org/p/cm/ld/fid=582). This is believed to be linked to several trends, ranging from what publishers are making available to readers liking the privacy that eBooks provide by shielding the book covers and titles from other people. Many science-fiction and fantasy readers are reported to having moved to preferring eBooks to physical books also (http://www.wired.com/2013/06/digital-publishing-genre-fiction/). It should be expected that reader preferences will continue to change and evolve, and there are many organizations creating surveys to capture the changes. Searching the Internet with texts like "who is reading eBooks?" will lead you to the latest discoveries in changes in reader behavior and the information can be folded into your library's eBook planning.

In addition to looking at what your patrons have shared with you, you can learn a lot by talking with colleagues in nearby library systems, or with libraries nationwide. There are conference sessions at regional and national library conferences as well as publishing conferences around a wide variety of topics related to eBooks. Just as publishers and other interested groups are surveying the public on reading preferences, libraries are sharing what they are learning about patron preference with regards to eBooks. What types of eBooks are proving most popular with their patrons, and what types don't seem to be circulating as well. What types of eBooks were tried that patrons did not check out. Connecting with libraries that serve similar patrons, and who work in the same type or similar size, will help to balance some of the broader "big picture" information trends with local details, which should help in designing an opening collection. This type of information might already be shared about print collections or other services, and this is just one more way to make a connection and share information and ideas as you start in this new area.

You'll also want to have a way to ask your patrons directly about their interests. If possible, we would suggest using at minimum two different methods—more if you have the time and resources. Here are some ideas on methods you might use to get you started:

- Create a short survey that is available on your website, as print copies at check-out stations, or as a bookmark that can be placed into reserved books. We have an example of a sample survey at the end of this chapter, in Figure 1.1.
- Ask your staff to gather information from your patrons during their interactions at your service desks. They can track comments and feedback from patrons about eBooks and eReaders that come up as part of their regular conversations about library materials. They could note when patrons ask them about eBooks, or they could ask directly about their interest when talking with them.
- Ask your volunteers or other committed library users from your community to participate in focus groups. An example of a committed library user group might be book club that meets at the library. Teen volunteers would make great focus groups, as would

retirees or others who are volunteering in your library. This is a great way to connect with the people who are already active supporters of the library about their interest in eBooks. Connecting with a variety of people will give you a great cross-section of thoughts and opinions.

- Create a special focus group to talk with about eBooks. This focus group could include people that you reach out to who are not regular users of your library, or who are only occasional users of library services. With this group, you are reaching patrons who may use the library in different ways than your volunteers or others who are active users and know a lot about what the library offers. They will give you a different insight than your active library supporters. They may even become active library supporters through this process.
- During outreach at a community event, have your survey or survey questions available. Don't miss an opportunity to connect at these types of events. You may find people here who aren't currently library users, but who may be interested in this new format and new way to connect with the library.

When beginning the process of offering eBooks, assess patron interest with a simple survey that asks a very basic question: "Would you be likely to use an eBook collection at the library?" The percentage of yes, no, or maybe will give a baseline estimate of your community's interest in using eBooks and can help to guide the planning process.

If you receive an overwhelming "yes" to your question, it may give you an idea about how quickly your patrons would like you to proceed with adding this new collection. It could be a sign that they're wondering why you don't have eBooks already, or that they're already purchasing eBooks from online retailers and would be happy to get books from the library also. They may already have devices, or may be comfortable with the technical skills they think they'll need. Maybe all of the children and teens in your community have school-issued tablets and are ready to use your collection, or maybe you have lots of business travelers who would like to have library eBooks available. Many communities with "snow birds," residents who move to a warmer climate in the winter months, have active eBook readers because they can use "their" library year-round by accessing their collections remotely when they're away from home. Whatever the reason for a lot of "yes" responses, you'll be able to move ahead knowing that there is patron interest, and possibly patron expectations, around your new collection.

A high percentage of "maybe" might lead you to ask some additional questions, since there may be some barriers to using eBooks that you'd like to know more about. Is there interest, but your patrons don't have devices, or don't know they can use many devices they may already have? Are they interested, but think they don't have the technical skills to check out books? Maybe they're interested, but don't know for sure that you'll have the books they're looking for? Knowing a little more about why people are interested but not sure that eBooks are for them will help you plan what types of promotion you'll need to do, and what types of staff and public training you'll want to consider, as you move ahead with your planning.

If you get a lot of "no" responses, you may want to take a step back and do some additional review here also. Some of the "no" responses may come from some of the same concerns as the "maybe" responses, with people thinking that they need to buy special equipment or need a high level of technical skills to use library eBooks. And some of the "no" responses could be from people who are genuinely not interested in eBooks, for a wide range of reasons. If most of your patrons let you know that they're not interested, and they're for reasons that you can't address with more complete or accurate information about how eBooks work, then you may want to consider your plan to move ahead at this point. While it seems unlikely that you'd end up with this situation, you'll want to consider what you'd do if your patrons told you that they didn't think they'd be interested in an eBook collection at your library. It may impact the speed with which you'd move ahead, the types of collection you'd purchase, or the types of community outreach you'd do.

In addition to gauging general interest in an eBook collection, there are three other areas where it would be helpful to have some information from your patrons:

- What do they want to read in eBook format?
- What device(s) do they have, or think they will be using?
- Who will be using the eBooks? What are the basic demographics about your potential users?

Knowing at least some basic information about the types of material your patrons would like to read in eBook format will, of course, be extremely helpful in setting up your initial collection. It will give you a place to start, especially if you have limited funds as most of us do when launching a new format. You'll be gathering some of that information as you review your current circulation and patron suggestion data, but you'll also want to ask your patrons directly about their interests. This will be especially true if you're trying to reach new users, who may not be showing up in your other data.

Knowing what devices your patrons are using will help you pick a library vendor for eBooks. While the major U.S. publishers are now working with a variety of library vendors, the devices that patrons are using most should be a factor in deciding with which vendor(s) to contract. Over time, the devices may become less of a factor as vendors are trending toward platforms that are device agnostic. However, in the current environment, some formats remain device-specific, so it is important to consider the device preferences of your patrons when selecting the vendor(s).

Acquiring demographic information can help in planning eBook collection. For example, if through the surveys you find that your patrons who express interest are primarily in the ages of 35–55 and have more interest in fiction than nonfiction, you can build your beginning collection targeting that group of patrons. This is also important if you're not sure if the primary users of your collection will be adults, or children and teens. You will need at least a basic understanding of who in your community is most likely to use your eBook collection. This may align with the information you have about who is using your print collection. But the answers may be quite different, depending on who in your community has (or is interested in having) the devices and general interest in eBooks.

As you develop your survey, remember to keep the survey short or your patrons may decline to participate. You're only looking for some high-level information here, and you're asking people to speculate about potential use of a collection that may not exist yet. Once you launch your new collection, you can continue to seek feedback from your patrons, but keep the survey short and easy to complete.

As you plan your eBook interest survey, strategize a number of ways to use it to reach a wide range of patrons. Providing a print copy of the survey for staff to give to patrons will be important. You should place copies in areas where patrons can pick them up independent of interactions with staff such as at self-check stations or in areas of the collection with heavy patron browsing traffic. Placing a survey as a bookmark within reserved books would reach patrons who place requests for books and may not browse the shelves. Also consider an online survey that can be used by patrons who visit your website and is included in your email newsletters or other outreach efforts. Since eBooks may have a special appeal to remote users (patrons who use your online resources, but may not visit the library frequently), take steps to ensure that your preliminary research survey reaches these users.

Data gathered in these ways will give an indication of what your patrons want (and perhaps don't want) and will provide a starting point for adding eBook services. As noted, eBooks, devices, and platforms change and shift rapidly. What device patrons are using today might not be the device of choice a year from now. But while the answers your patrons give you now may not hold true for long, the information will give you a way to start an eBook service. Because of the frequent changing and shift in devices, patron behavior, and the like, track which data points were used and the way the data was collected in this initial phase. You can reuse the methodology at a later date when you want to evaluate your collection and service with an eye to expand or reshape it.

Planning the Service You Will Offer

Figuring out how to get started with a new collection or new format is always a challenge. There really is no quick and easy way to do it, because it's dependent on the community you serve and the resources you have available. That said, libraries have always added new formats as they've become available, and eBooks are simply part of that story. Tackling eBooks the same way your library has added other formats in the past will help your staff and patrons understand this transition.

Once data has been collected, collated, and analyzed, it's time to start developing a scope of service. While your patrons may have a wide range of reading interests and use many different devices, there will likely be some trends in the surveys and other feedback channels to help your staff determine where to begin.

Identifying Your Target Audience

To get started, you need to identify some target audiences for the launch of the service. Based on the data collected, should a primary focus be to reach adult fiction readers, but not necessarily patrons looking for cookbooks and home improvement? Or have all of the students in your service area received tablets from their school, and will focusing on homework and recreational resources for them be your focus? While you may have the budgetary and staff resources to serve multiple audiences, you may still want to start with one or more target groups like adult fiction readers and homework and recreational reading support for students in grades 6–12. With key patron groups in mind, you'll be able to test your service plan and collection development needs against some real "readers" with specific types of needs.

Focusing on a small number of target audiences will help in evaluating the use of the collection after it has been launched. If a target audience is adult fiction readers, and a beginning collection has been purchased to reach that audience, evaluating the success of the collection becomes easier. Having a category that's too broad, like "library patrons" or "adults" will make it much more difficult to determine whom you are reaching and what adjustments you may want to make in your purchasing or marketing. Take time to think through and identify which key groups of patrons you wish to reach first.

After determining the initial group of target audiences, it's helpful to create talking points for staff, because they most likely will receive questions from interested patrons asking, "Why don't you have _____?" Staff will want to be able to talk about what's in the beginning collection and whom you are hoping to reach. You'll also want to create a way for staff to capture suggestions from patrons as they are interacting with them, so they don't miss a chance to document patron suggestions about what they would like to see included in your eBook collection.

Engaging Stakeholders

In addition to checking in with your patrons about their interest in eBooks, you'll want to ensure your library administration, library board or trustees, and other key stakeholders are engaged and are invited to provide input. These groups should be included in your general survey and feedback process. You will also want to know of any goals or needs they may have as you start and develop your eBook collection and service. If they are especially interested in specific areas—increasing circulation, connecting with schools or senior centers, or expanding online service—you'll want to make sure you can speak to their interests as the service plan is being created.

Library staff are also stakeholders. Your library administration, library board, or trustees may have specific outcomes in mind, like an interest in circulation or connecting with schools or senior centers. And because of their positions in the library, their needs will be incorporated into the planning. But library staff should also be included in the process, as their interactions with patrons are a key to a successful launch and they can provide feedback as to obstacles they see in providing eBooks to patrons.

It is easy to forget your stakeholders in your planning process because they may be less likely to be considered a "user" of the collection in the traditional sense. Library board members may not be interested in reading library eBooks themselves, so they are not interested in what titles you are buying, but they are interested in whether circulation has increased because the library has added eBooks to its collection. Library staff may be more interested in exactly what eBook titles are being purchased because they are responding to individual patron inquiries. But they may not necessarily be concerned with reaching a certain target circulation figure. Being aware of stakeholder interests and definitions of success, like an increase in circulation or having particular titles from the beginning, will help you address questions and concerns as they arise. Keeping stakeholders interested may potentially secure additional funding, and is a key part of developing advocates and supporters of this new or expanded service.

Assembling Your Planning Team

Preparing to launch or expand an eBook collection is a complex process. You must consider a wide range of technical details. You must also look at the overall patron experience as well as the impact on your staff, selection, and online services. It's easy to think of your eBook launch as a collection management issue, and that's the traditional way that these types of initiatives have been approached in libraries. Your library is adding a new format or type of collection, so your collection staff roll out the new materials. In many cases, that process has worked just fine. The impact on other parts of your library system may have been minimal; your staff may not have needed additional training, and your patrons may have started to use them with little impact on your staff or broader library processes.

We'd suggest that the implementation of an eBook collection is best managed with a more inclusive approach that includes a wide mix of staff. Your eBook collection is not only a collection of titles. Launching an eBook service will have a definite impact on overall patron service. The new service will affect the types of questions patrons ask as they try to access library materials, the way you support readers and researchers of all ages, the way you support your online resources, and your technical and desktop support. You may also need to evaluate your library collection development and other policies as you move ahead with your eBook collection. While the types of changes that are needed will be specific to your library, you should consider these various areas as you start your planning.

Pulling together a cross-functional team to lead your process will help you work through a wider range of issues as you get started, and will also hopefully lead to having more staff invested in the outcome for your patrons. By using a cross-functional team, your eBook launch won't be something that "happened" to your public services staff, and it won't be something that your technical team won't understand or know how to support. Having a mix of people involved will allow you to get ahead of the challenges such as staff training, and you may be able to prepare ahead of launch for any public programs or training sessions you'll want to provide. This cross-functional group will also help you develop your marketing and promotional strategy, and talk through questions about the use of statistics and other information you'll want to use as you move ahead.

This is a model that you can use no matter the size of your library. Even a smaller library can work collaboratively with a few key staff so that the launch of an eBook collection is not the work of just one person. A small group of 2–3 people, representing your key areas (patron service, collection, technology), will get more voices and perspectives into the planning process. For larger libraries or library systems, having several people representing various aspects of patron service, collection, and technology is advised. If you work in a large system and have a large number of staff, or multiple branches, it's easy for your staff to not feel connected or represented in launching a service like eBooks. Having a more inclusive, team approach will help make sure more perspectives, including those from staff who work directly with your patrons, will be at the table. Having these perspectives at the table may help you avoid potential hurdles or complications as you design your service.

Of course, it's possible that not everyone will see their role in this type of work. As we noted, these types of changes have often been led solely by collection staff, and other staff may be surprised to be included, and may not clearly see their role here. This may be especially true for staff who don't fully understand the complexity that eBooks can bring to your library. Your technical team may not know that some eBook lending models require users to download software to access the books. As well as users, your technical team may also need to help library staff to download software for training purposes, and possibly support users when they come to the library to access the eBook collection. Or this may be the first time your library decides to buy tablets or eReaders, and you'll then need to set up and maintain these devices, which may be new to your technical team. In addition, many libraries don't have their own technical staff, but work with their city, county, or other group for this type of support. Having these shared staff be part of your eBook team can be an additional complication, but one that's worth trying to resolve to get ahead of any support issues needed for your staff or patrons.

However you approach it, bringing together a cross-functional team of staff at the start of your project will give you a leg up on your planning. And if you don't start with this type of team, it's never too late to bring more staff together as you move into maintaining your collection. More staff may want to be part of the conversation as your service develops, and they see a clearer role and ways to improve service for your patrons.

CONCLUSION

There are many considerations as you plan to implement a new eBook collection, or add to an existing service, and we'll be covering them in the next chapters. eBooks for library patrons exist in an environment with many variables, including changes in publishing, vendor options, and reader preferences. Discovering the interests and expectations of your patrons is crucial. Looking at current use of your collections, what patrons wish they could check out from the library if only it were available, direct patron feedback from surveys or conversation, and stakeholder needs and wants will give you the information necessary to determine who are the initial target audiences for the collection and what types of eBooks will be in the collection at launch. Also plan at the outset about how you'll continue to connect with your users as your service develops, for example, another survey or focus group conversation, how to measure your success, and how you'll integrate eBooks into your other work processes.

While it may all seem overwhelming, taking the time to create a plan will help you get started on the right foot with this new adventure.

Our library is considering adding eBooks to our collection. We'd like to hear from you about your interest in eBooks and what devices you'd be using to read eBooks from the library's collection.

Would you be interested in our library system offering eBooks?
- Yes, definitely
- Maybe, I might read them
- No, I don't read eBooks

Would you be reading eBooks primarily for:
- School/homework
- Recreation or leisure
- Work topics
- Research

How do you currently read eBooks? Circle all that apply
- On a cell phone
  - iOS/iPhone
  - Android
- On a tablet
  - iPad
  - Surface
  - Kindle (the tablet ones)
- On a dedicated eReader
  - Kindle
  - Nook
  - Kobo
  - Other

Figure 1.1   Sample Patron Survey

- On a desktop computer or laptop
  - iOS/Mac
  - PC
- Other types of device

What types of eBooks would you be interested in reading? Circle all that apply.
- Romance
- Mystery
- Science Fiction
- Fantasy
- Thrillers
- Horror
- Western
- Literary
- Self-help
- Cookbooks
- Biographies
- Travel
- Religion
- History

What is your age range? (optional)
- 12–14
- 15–17
- 18–25
- 26–35
- 36–55
- 56–65
- 66–75
- 76–85
- 86+

Thank you for taking a few moments to give us your feedback. We appreciate it!

Figure 1.1   (Continued)

CHAPTER 2

How Did We Get Here?

When looking at all of the technical parts and pieces that need to be in place for anyone to read a book on a device, it is quite amazing. The goal of this chapter is to give you an idea of all of the components that have developed in a relatively short space of time that make it possible for libraries to provide eBooks to their patrons. The complexity of what needed to be developed so that eBooks could become an important part of the publishing landscape, as well as a viable option as a format for libraries, is important to understand. While you don't need to have exhaustive knowledge of all of the components, even a general understanding will be valuable as your library launches or expands an eBook collection.

In Chapter 3 we describe several options that are available for providing eBooks to your patrons: free eBooks, building your own system, or contracting with a vendor or vendors. No matter which option or options you choose for your library, the basic elements we discuss in this chapter will need to be present for your system to work well for your users. Having a basic understanding of the fundamental components of how these parts work together will help you make technical decisions, as well as help you determine which of the options will help your library meet your service goals. There may be elements you would like to handle at your library and ones you might like to contract to a vendor, or ways you can combine local and vendor options to meet your needs. Developing a basic knowledge will also allow you to make informed decisions going forward as the eBook publishing and technical environment continues to change and as your user needs and expectations change over time. To help you track all of the areas to consider, you will find a checklist of the key areas helpful as you start your planning. You'll find a sample checklist at the end of this chapter (Figure 2.1).

DEVICES, CONTENT, AND READING EXPERIENCE

The first dedicated eReaders were developed in the late 1990s. As is often the case with new technologies, these first devices garnered a small following, but didn't expand to mainstream use. It wasn't until the 2000s that dedicated devices that captured the attention and interest of a wider audience were developed. These second-generation devices were compact, light, and attractive, at least by the standards of their times. They may seem large and cumbersome when compared to current devices, but for the times, these devices met the criteria that users were looking for; the devices provided a new and enticing way for general readers to connect with books.

For this more mainstream consumer audience, an eBook reader needed to be an object they would be interested in owning, ideally: attractive, not too big, and not too heavy. Other consumer devices in the marketplace at that time were getting smaller. Developers were improving designs on all types of devices to make them more attractive to use, and eReaders were part of that trend. Once users had a device they would be willing to carry with them as well as a method to put an eBook onto the device, the reading experience had to be one that they would enjoy. The eBook had to look good on the screen. The text had to be clear and legible. In short, it had to be as good as, or at least close to, the experience of reading a physical book. For example, readers had an expectation that they could turn "pages" of a book smoothly, because that's how they were used to moving ahead in a physical book.

Readers quickly added other expectations to what they wanted to have available when reading an eBook. For example, physical books let readers use bookmarks or turn down page corners to remember where they left off reading. Being able to put down a book and start up again in the same place is an expected part of the reading experience. Being able to "bookmark" where they stopped reading in an eBook soon became a function that readers fully expected to have available. Starting at the beginning of the digital file each time they picked up the eReader was unacceptable to the average reader. Another standard expectation for an eReader is that the text be legible in bright light and low light, since eBooks can be read in bed as well as on the beach. Being able to adjust the font size and style has also quickly become a basic expectation for readers when selecting an eReader. Not all of this functionality existed with the earlier eReaders, which is part of what limited their appeal to a broader audience. As these reader-friendly areas improved and more closely aligned with what readers were used to already with print books, the eReaders sparked the interest of more potential users.

Another expectation from readers was related to the size of the device itself. The eBook reader needed to be small and light enough that it was easy to carry throughout the day. It had to be light enough to hold in reader's hands for potentially long lengths of time while they were reading. If the device was too heavy or too bulky, it wouldn't meet the needs of many readers who would expect to be able to use it to read for more than a few minutes at a time, or when reading on the train or relaxing on the back porch. The battery had to last long enough to read at least a few hours, or ideally to read a few books, without needing to be recharged. If a reader had the backlighting on or was using some of the other added functionality, the battery had to support that use as well without running down.

Beyond the physical size of the device itself, storage capacity for the device was also important. The eReader had to have enough capacity to allow the user to store many eBooks. The early eReaders could only hold a few books, usually under a dozen. Being able to store only a few books wasn't that much of an advantage over physical books, and was part of the limited appeal of the earliest devices. Storage for enough books to take on a trip, or to keep all of the books that had been purchased, was an important advantage of the eReader, and as that capacity expanded, the devices became more appealing. And of course, if a user wanted to purchase an eBook and add it to his or her device, the process had to be easy and virtually instantaneous, ideally using wireless connections so a book could be added to the device at any time.

As consumers became more intrigued by eReaders and the eBook reading experience matured, the major U.S. book publishers began their own forays into eBooks. The publishers worked in two main tracks: by publishing new titles in an eBook version as well as in print and by converting their backlist to eBooks. Now there were both devices that appealed to consumers and content that a broader range of the reading public was interested in. As we mentioned in Chapter 1, the concept of an eBook or online book or electronic book had been around for at least a decade or more before the explosion into the consumer market, but the content of those e-versions of books was intended for specific audiences rather than mass appeal. The move from publishing for smaller niche markets to current, popular titles and backlist titles is an important part of what has made eBooks much more interesting for libraries and our patrons.

As eBooks gained popularity with a broader audience, publishers of other types of material looked at eReaders and wondered if there was a market for their content in this new world. Magazine and newspaper publishers, publishers of picture books and textbooks, comic book publishers, and others began to see new opportunities also. As the reading experience has improved with new generations of eReaders and other devices, more publishers have started bringing a wider range of materials to the marketplace. These new types of materials have helped drive changes to eReaders and other devices, and have also continued to expand the appeal for users.

With the increasing development of appealing devices, expanded content, and the improved reading experience came a proliferation of companies looking to become part of this growing market, which led to more players developing and selling both eReaders and related devices and online content. Many traditional bricks-and-mortar bookstores as well as online bookstores have embraced eReaders and eBooks, looking for ways to bring a new reading experience to their customers. Some library vendors have even developed their own proprietary devices for libraries to offer to their patrons, stepping beyond their usual role of only selling or licensing the books or other content to libraries.

Amazon's first Kindle eReader was released in late 2007 and was an instant hit with readers, selling out within a few hours of going on sale. This first Kindle could hold approximately 200 titles (without illustrations.) Amazon has developed many versions of eReaders since then, and its primary eReader product today is a tablet with a touch screen. These newer devices are not only capable of handling illustrations, but they are also able to stream movies and music. Barnes & Noble's first Nook eReader was introduced in 2009. This first Nook had a 2 GB storage and weighed 12.1 ounces. Barnes & Noble's current Nook products are now a little over 6 ounces and have 4 GB of storage. Apple introduced its first tablet, the iPad, in 2010. It weighed more than the Kindles and Nooks, coming in at around 1.5 pounds, but had substantially more storage and provided much more functionality than a basic eReader. Apple launched the iPad knowing that it too wanted to sell eBooks to consumers, as well as provide a wider range of services than a device just aimed at reading books could offer. Apple launched iBooks, its online bookstore, at the same time as it launched the iPad. The iBooks store started with 60,000 titles from major

U.S. publishers. In only five years since the launch of iBooks, Apple now says it has over 2.5 million titles available for purchase, and the new devices it has launched since the first iPad have expanded in functionality also.

These are examples of products from only three of the companies selling eReaders and eBooks to consumers and the massive changes that have happened within just a few years. Current eReaders and related devices are expected to hold hundreds of titles, and be able to display a large number of pictures and other images. Expectations for the optimal size of screen for reading can still vary widely, as the devices can be used for reading books as well as other functions, and are used in many types of settings. Like cell phones, screen sizes for tablets and eReaders are changing in response to consumer feedback. Regardless of the size of device, consumers have a strong expectation that the device is light and easy to store and carry. The Nook's loss of 4 ounces in terms of weight from the earliest models to the ones in the market today is significant, since making the current generations of devices easy to hold has proven to be important for users. Apple's bookstore now holds 98% more titles than it did at launch, and other booksellers have also increased their inventory significantly, since readers want a wide selection of materials to choose from. Before there were actual books to read, there was not a compelling reason to purchase an eReader, and one less reason to purchase a tablet or similar device.

Improvements, changes, updates, and experiments with devices and the reading experience continue to shift and change with amazing rapidity. As the eBook revolution started, there was reluctance or uncertainty from publishers of all sizes about how best to enter the eBook market. Now virtually all U.S. publishers provide an eBook version of their new titles for readers to purchase from online retailers and to make available to library vendors for sale to libraries. In fact, some publishers are starting to publish an eBook-only version of some titles and subjects rather than publishing a physical version, based on what they're seeing readers prefer. It has taken a few years, but many publishers are now working with library vendors to allow their content to be licensed to libraries and be lent to patrons.

The devices, the reading experience, the content, and easy ways to access that content have definitely developed to an extent that a broad consumer audience, not just the early adopters of technology, are interested. Because there wasn't (and isn't now) just one device, one reading experience, or one place that patrons were and are obtaining eBooks, there are parts that are "under the hood" that will be helpful to understand as your library considers starting or expanding your collection. This background will help you understand the key components of the eBook experience as you move across all of the options available to your library.

PROTECTING THE CONTENT: DRM AND FILE TYPES

While publishers want their content to be purchased and read by as many people as possible, they also want to try to protect their digital content. Digital files work differently than physical books, and many publishers are concerned that an eBook file is not simply purchased once and then copied countless times by an unlimited number of people. They are concerned about any way that individual users can pass digital copies around without ever needing to purchase a new copy. This can include a user uploading of an eBook file to a file-sharing network accessible to anyone with an Internet connection, or files being shared between readers through other methods like copying to a thumb drive.

One of the more challenging issues for users and publishers is related to the ways that print books work differently from digital copies of books. Print books have always been able to be shared. They're usually small, portable, and easy to share one-to-one with another potential user. One reader, or one library, can purchase the book and loan it, or give it, to others to read, and that new user can pass it on to another user. And this model is actually covered in U.S. copyright law: 17 U.S.C. § 109: US Code—Section 109: Limitations on exclusive rights: Effect of transfer of particular copy or phonorecord (http://codes .lp.findlaw.com/uscode/17/1/109#sthash.C6iUQtfC.dpuf).

While publishers would probably prefer that every user purchased their own copy of the books they read, the ability to loan and share print books is part of the long, and understood, process of how "ownership" works in that environment. And part of why it works is that the physical copy of the book will eventually wear out and need to be replaced, or purchased again, if new users want to read it. You can loan a book to a few people, but something will probably happen to that copy: someone will spill coffee on it, tear out a few pages, or leave it on the bus. Even if none of these more dire things befall a print book, it's likely that through repeated reading the book will eventually wear out and another copy can be sold to replace it. Libraries can lend their copies of *To Kill a Mockingbird* to students reading it for their English class, but will probably need to buy a few more copies so next year's class can read it too. But digital copies don't wear out, and don't need to be replaced the same way. If you leave your eReader on the bus, you still have the file because you have purchased it virtually and once you have a new device you can download the file again. Your English class won't need new copies of the book for the class assignment next year because the copies you purchased this year are still all in perfect condition on your library's digital bookshelf. This might be a positive change for users, but presents some challenges for publishers, as well as for the authors themselves, who are often paid by the number of copies of their books that are sold.

Enter digital rights management, or DRM. DRM seeks to control the access to digital material through technical means. What that means for libraries in simplified and practical terms is that there is a layer of software that is managing what a consumer or library patron can do with the eBook once they have it. For instance, it may be possible for a consumer to print part or even all of the eBook if he or she wants to depending on the DRM that has been applied, or printing may be limited or prohibited based on the rights that are assigned to the digital file. DMR dictates the number of devices the consumer or library patron can access the file on: phones, computers, dedicated eReaders, and others. Depending on the rights assigned, a user can download a file to an unlimited number or type of devices, or may only be able to use it on a specific type of device, or a total of 2, 3, or 4 devices before the access is restricted. DRM can also count how many times a digital file like an eBook can be used or lent before additional access is denied. It scopes and manages access to the digital file, setting parameters about how a user can use the digital file.

A natural tension exists here between those who create the content, own the copyright, or provide access to the content and those who purchase or otherwise access the material. Users want, need, and demand to have flexibility as to how, when, how much, and on which devices they use digital material, in our case, eBooks. Publishers and authors, the owners of the copyright, acknowledge that consumers who have purchased the material want and need to have to have flexibility, but they don't want to give away so much flexibility that they lose sales and their product becomes devalued. There are pressures on all sides to provide increased access and flexibility for digital materials. But the providers also seek to ensure that those who create the works (authors), and make the works available for users (publishers), are compensated for their work, and that relevant copyright and other laws are followed throughout the process.

That said, there are currently some publishers experimenting with providing DRM-free access to their digital material. They're doing this for a number of reasons. Sometimes the reasons are philosophical; not all publishers and authors believe that DRM is the right approach to the challenge they are facing, and don't believe that there should be barriers of this sort between the content and the user. Sometimes the reasons for allowing DRM-free access are more practical. They hear from many users and potential users who would like to purchase or otherwise access their materials but who find the additional steps needed to access content with DRM unnecessarily complicated, limiting potential sales to these users. Instead of staying with the current DRM model, some publishers and authors are working to establish a business model in this new environment with the belief that most users won't use free file-sharing, but will still prefer to purchase and own their own copies of digital materials. They're looking for a model that limits illegal or unwanted file-sharing, but that doesn't have such a negative impact on the average user who is legally accessing material and not using file-sharing or other processes. However, most major U.S. publishers currently do impose access limitations by using DRM. This includes often limiting the number of devices that can access the same file while checked out to a single user, which allows some flexibility but yet still constrains overall access.

In addition to DRM, file types are used to control the use of material. Device producers, especially dedicated eReader devices makers, can dictate which file type or types can be used on their devices. While many devices work with a wide range of file types, this is not always the case. And eBook retailers, including those that also sell proprietary devices like Amazon with their Kindle products, are especially interested in also developing and maintaining a proprietary file type. They are seeking to create a reading experience so complete and attractive that the consumer is not tempted to leave their retail space to purchase different devices or eBooks from any other seller. You can buy the book and the device from the same place and know that they will work seamlessly together. It may not be as easy, or even possible, to use the books you purchase from one vendor on other devices and your device may work less smoothly with books you obtain from other sources, but that ideally keeps you going back to the vendor that works most consistently for you. Amazon, with its Kindle family of devices and its proprietary file type AZW, is an example of this model. Barnes & Noble, with its Nook device, is an example of a model that aligns a vendor device and online bookstore model, but doesn't use a proprietary file type model. Barnes & Noble would obviously prefer that its customers buy all of its eBooks from it, but it is not using a file type that works only on its Nook devices, or that can be purchased only from its online bookstore.

Besides Amazon's proprietary AZW file types, two of the other most common file types are EPUB and PDF. Both are stable, widely used file types for eBooks, and are considered the international industry standards at this time. Both provide a standardized and consistent way to manage a range of content types, and work across a wide range of eReaders and other devices. The EPUB file type is a *free* and *open* standard created by the International Digital Publishing Forum. EPUB stands for Electronic Publication, and is used widely by eBook publishers. PDF, which stands for portable document format, was originally a proprietary format developed by Adobe, and was developed to allow users to share documents regardless of software, hardware, or operating systems. PDF has since moved from being a proprietary format to an open format like EPUB. Both of these formats are now open standards, hence their appeal as file types to use to publish eBooks.

As eBooks began to be published, most text-based books used EPUB, and there was a tendency for books like picture books, with lots of images, to use the PDF format. The PDF format presented the full picture in a similar manner as the physical version. The complete image which is so important in books like picture books was provided intact rather than split across several screens. It was seen as a format that provided a comparable experience to the print book experience. The disadvantage of using the PDF format is that it does not scale itself to the smaller screens of mobile devices. It works as hoped with devices like desktop or laptop computers and tablets with larger screens, but doesn't provide the desired experience with the newer, smaller devices. While PDF books are still available through library and other vendors, they are not used as widely as EPUB for most types of eBooks now that more patrons are using devices that don't maximize the benefits of this format.

EPUB and its DRM-free companion file type, Open EPUB, are the most commonly used nonproprietary file types for eBooks at this time. These file types allow for ease of transfer to many types of devices. EPUB and Open EPUB provide a reading experience that gives the reader the ability to bookmark pages, highlight text, and adjust fonts and font size. Since EPUB has DRM and DRM-free options, it can provide a consistent reader experience with DRM applied or without DRM. By DRM of the file, we mean the limits set by a publisher as to how many devices the file can be transferred to, how many pages can be printed, and so on. As patrons begin to understand file types, they understand what their reading experience will be like as they choose the file type from the options available to them.

In addition to file types, device operating systems play a part in how all of these components work together. Perhaps the best thing to be said is that at least at the moment, there are only two main operating systems to contend with, iOS and Android, which are used by the majority of devices. iOS is the operating system for Apple products, while Android is the operating system developed by Google. The operating systems provide yet another level of complexity for eBook users because any eBook software needs to work with the architecture of the operating system. Software developers therefore have to make two versions of all software, one that will run with Android and one version that will run using iOS. The operating system issue doesn't have the same impact as some of the other variables in eBook access because Android and iOS are the current de facto standards. This means that software is being produced so that eBook systems will run using either operating system. Having two standard operating systems is yet another part of the complex system that's in place to support eBook use for the general reader.

Just as is happening with changes to devices, there are and will continue to be modifications and developments being made to file types to make them usable in the widest variety of devices and with the widest variety of contents. While there will be adjustments and updates to operating systems, it is unlikely that we will see the standard shrink to only one system. But as the use of eBooks grows and matures, patrons are increasingly interested in reading a wider range of materials, including fiction, picture books, nonfiction, comics, manga, magazines, and other popular materials, in these formats. Will there one day be a single file type that can provide an optimal experience for all of this disparate content? Perhaps, but then the devices will have to be made or adjusted to accommodate the file type and the retailers who want to keep their customers in a controlled environment will have to decide whether it's worth adopting.

Lending eBooks

DRM and file types protect access to eBooks for publishers and authors, no matter where the books are made available. Now add into the mix libraries that would like to lend eBooks, not just provide a single user/provider retail-style transaction, and you are adding yet another layer of complexity and rights management to the eBook world. At present, the way the library lending model works is to parallel as much as possible the ways libraries lend physical books. Libraries buy (or buy access to) a book, inventory it so we can track it, lend it out for a certain period of time, and expect that it is returned. While there are some differences in the way this actually works for physical copies of books and for eBooks, in design, both models work the same way, with the same underlying expectations.

Library vendors, and some library systems that have developed their own platforms, have created software that will put all of the necessary mechanisms into place to allow libraries to lend materials and for them to be returned for another use. The software limits the number of checkouts per patron, the length of time a book can be on loan, the ability to place a hold on eBooks, and the process for returning an eBook once the loan period is completed. Because this lending experience is happening virtually, the checkout and return process is handled by inserting an expiration date into the file that the patron checks out. The book essentially returns itself; in most cases access to the file expires, and the patron doesn't need to do anything to "return" the book. All the patron needs to do is delete the file from his or her device when prompted by the software. Those are the basics of lending needed by libraries. But libraries provide a host of other services to our patrons, and we needed a whole suite of other services to be developed as well.

In our libraries, we create and organize physical books into smaller collections from the multitudes of books published and potentially available to our users. This is, of course, exactly the same in the eBook world. In order to make materials available to our users, we needed robust software from library vendors, or from the platforms we've built ourselves, to allow us to easily choose materials from the wide variety of options available from publishers. We needed ways to manage holds and holds lists since we may need to limit the number of eBooks a patron can have at one time. Our patrons may want a mechanism to identify books they want to read, but aren't ready to check out yet. We also pride ourselves on describing and classifying material, putting similar materials together on reader-friendly lists or grouping books by subject so it's easy to find all the books on a specific topic.

In response to these needs, library vendors built holds management tools for us, built wishlist capabilities for patrons, and gave us the ability to highlight eBook titles in featured reading lists. Vendors implemented cataloging options, either ways for libraries to create MARC records, and/or facilitated the purchase of fully cataloged MARC records from yet other vendors. Besides all these services that libraries might call basic options, vendors are constantly developing more functionality for their products. They are in conversations with library staff talking about what functionality patrons are looking for as well as analyzing what is happening in the general marketplace. Vendors are offering functionality that we may not initially thought of as important or of interest to our patrons but, upon investigation and implementation, becomes useful and valuable to patrons. More about options that vendors offer will be discussed in later chapters, but one example of this functionality is the ability to link patrons to a bookseller of choice via a "buy it now" button, directing patrons to ways to easily purchase an eBook if a library copy isn't available, or if they'd rather own than borrow a copy of the book.

Discovery and Access

Yet another piece needed in the library lending model is a "place" for your library's collection to live independently that is unique from any other library's collection. This means a website or other access devoted to an individual library's collection that's separate from what might be available from another library. This website needs to both acknowledge the vendor (if you are using one) and the library system that is providing the specific books on the site. It needs to have excellent searching capabilities, comparable to what your patrons are used to from your general library catalog, or from online bookstores. Patrons want to find the content they are interested in quickly and with a minimum of clicks. The website will need to be optimized to work on any type of device, or with a separate app that supports access on multiple devices.

Often the website needs to interact with authentication software based on any limitations a library needs. You or your library system, if you are a part of one, may want or need to restrict who will use an eBook collection, based on contractual agreements with publishers or for funding reasons. Or perhaps you want to limit the eBook collection to patrons under a designated fine threshold. To be able to limit access with these types of restrictions, authentication software needs to be employed. When a patron enters his or her library barcode in order to check out or request an eBook, there is often software running in the background which is checking both to see if the barcode is valid and to see if the patron is in good standing, based on the criteria established by the library. Ideally, the authentication software should be invisible and instantaneous to the patrons, so they aren't slowed down in their search for eBooks. If the patron is refused access to the collection or denied the ability to check out eBook titles, the messages returned to the patron should be written in plain language and easily understandable.

Once the patron is through the authentication process, the website needs to facilitate the next steps in the library lending process, particularly checkout and holds. These functions need to operate in a quick and easy manner, so the patron is able to browse for and obtain the materials he or she is looking for. The website should be a place where patrons can manage their "account" with the library, which includes all of the parts that they want to manage as part of their eBook experience, particularly what they have checked out. Patrons want to know when their eBooks will expire and if they can return their eBooks early, as they're used to doing with the physical items they've checked out from the library. Patrons also want to manage lists of titles that they are waiting for and a want place to keep a list of what they may be interested in checking out in the future, creating a wishlist of future books to read.

Even though it may seem like many of these applications have been around for as long as dedicated eReaders, in reality, these applications have become ubiquitous only within the past few years. Libraries now expect vendors to have attractive and easily used online tools for their products, because that's what your patrons expect. Users are looking for an easy-to-use online experience that makes getting an eBook onto their device as simple as possible. That ease of use needs to align with what they're used to when using other parts of your collections and services and also needs to align with the experience they have in an online retail environment.

To make access to your library eBook collection possible there needs to be at least basic website access to the collection. Ideally, the website would use responsive design, allowing it to work across desktop, laptop, and mobile interfaces with the same user experience. Unfortunately, this isn't always in place for library or vendor websites. Much of the reading experience today is wireless and mobile. Therefore individual vendor apps also need to be available to support the mobile experience and provide access on mobile devices. Apps can provide access to the library or vendor collection, and can also provide the reading platform which allows the eBook to be opened and read. This again is a reminder that the story of eBooks is increasingly mobile, as readers expect to be able to bring their devices, and access their eBooks, from wherever they happen to be when they're ready to read. Dedicated eReaders are still here, but the growth and the focus of eBooks with relation to devices has increasingly turned to smartphones and tablets. These types of devices have proliferated in the marketplace, and consumers of eBooks are using their smartphones and tablets as a favorite place to read eBooks. They're becoming less interested in carrying two devices, one to read eBooks and one to read everything else. This type of change is indicative of the changes under way in this broader world that librarians are working in, and will be the type of change to watch for as you're adding or expanding your eBook collection.

Storage of eBooks and Access to eBook Files

The role of the library or vendor website or separate app is to give your patrons the information they need regarding the eBooks in your collection. It's the catalog, the discovery layer, the searching or browsing experience. In the general marketplace, it's where customers learn what is available for them to check out, now or at a later date. But where are the actual eBooks?

Because the eBooks themselves aren't taking up physical shelf space, it's easy to overlook this aspect of the eBook landscape. The eBooks or files do have to live somewhere. That somewhere is on servers that are owned and managed by someone, and all storage comes with a cost. If you decide to contract with a vendor to offer eBooks, this is one of pieces you are paying the vendor to take care of for you. If you decide to create and host your own service, this is one of the pieces you will need to oversee, administer, and pay for. The files that your patrons will be downloading or otherwise accessing will need to be stored by you, or by your vendors, and then moved from your storage to their devices.

Vendors manage this movement from their storage to user devices in a number of ways. This process currently varies by vendor, so your patrons may have to use more than one way to get eBooks from your library if you are using more than one platform. Many library vendors are using a process that has a patron move the file from the vendor storage to his or her device by using Adobe software, which the patron will need to set up before he or she can actually get access to the books. While there needs to be a way to move the files from one place to another, this step is considered cumbersome by many users, and can be a barrier for many to actually get the eBooks to their devices. And with each vendor approaching this step differently, that can add complexity to the process also.

CONCLUSION

Among the many moving parts involved in the way eBooks actually work for libraries and the broader eBook world are devices, content, reading experience, DRM, file types, the library lending experience, websites, and apps. These are all layered on top of and through each other. How they all interact with each other is what makes the whole process work. When you tease apart the world of eBooks, it is astounding that all of the pieces have developed into a system that not only works, but that it has only existed in its current form for a few years.

The model discussed in this chapter provides an overview of the most common trends and practices in the current library/publisher/vendor/reader model. But in many ways it's still an uneasy alliance between the parties. It serves the needs of all to some extent, but no one really is happy with the complete package. Many readers, authors, libraries, and publishers are unsatisfied with the current DRM model. The current DRM model can create additional steps and barriers for getting the books into the hands, or onto the devices, of the people who want to read the books, and who have the legal right to have access to the material. In addition, many other individuals and organizations do not support DRM on philosophical or legal grounds. There are questions of rights, access, and funding behind some of these concerns, and the way digital rights are currently managed is probably only a temporary process on the path to a more comprehensive solution.

And as you know or will learn, this is not solely an eBook issue, or a library concern. DRM in its many forms applies to a much broader range of materials, including music, film and video, and other digital content and tools. There are changes and challenges happening in each of those unique environments. While the issues being addressed are essentially the same, the discussion around the business, legal, and technical needs and concerns will vary by industry. This continues to be a somewhat-contentious conversation across the world of digital content. This discussion is one that librarians who offer eBooks or other digital content, or that are considering doing so, should continue to follow, at least at a high level. Changes in the way DRM is handled in the music world, or with film and video, could have a ripple effect in the way it is handled by eBook publishers, vendors, and device manufacturers, which could lead to changes in the way libraries offer eBooks to their patrons. The following of trends is covered again in Chapter 8.

This does not mean that your library system shouldn't consider launching an eBook collection. Providing content with DRM as well as DRM-free materials for your library patrons can still be a fairly straightforward process regardless of whether you work with vendors or are creating your own system. This is just another part of the eBook environment that remains in flux in the broader national and international development and expansion of access to digital content, and that is not solely a library issue.

Because there are so many parts to the eBook system, there are almost unlimited possibilities to make improvements in the technology. You'll learn more about what you might expect to see change and develop throughout the rest of the book, but there are a couple of themes we expect to emerge as the technology is redesigned: simplicity of access and format agnosticism. One example of simplicity is exemplified by the customer expectations that the entire process of obtaining an eBook will happen in as few clicks as possible. The fewer the clicks, the more seamless the experience. It doesn't mean that any of the steps are necessarily going away, but more and more may be happening in the background once a customer or patron makes just one click. The fewer the clicks, the more sales likely for a bookstore and the more checkouts for a library. An example of device and format agnosticism is an expectation that there will be companies trying to improve the proprietary model by making or allowing content to be used on any device, regardless of operating system. Companies with proprietary file types would obviously prefer that customers stay within the system they have built. However, if a file type is developed that is deemed an improvement over the file type offered by the proprietary company, customers will move their business. As said earlier, it is doubtful that the two operating system worlds will reduce to one or be replaced by a new one, but with technology, obviously anything is possible. Currently there is more potential that there will be changes in the process (fewer clicks) and more standardization and improvements in file types. Since libraries serve such a wide range of patrons who bring every type of device ever made into our libraries, having anyone who could reduce the number of variables (like file types) would be advantageous.

As talked about in Chapter 1, you want to discover what devices your patrons are currently using to read and purchase eBooks. Having that information will help you navigate through the technical components we just discussed. As you consider how you will offer eBooks to your patrons, you have some options in terms of technology. While all the parts we described earlier need to be present, some will be provided by the patrons. They will most likely be providing the reading device, whether computer, smart phone, or eReader. Some libraries do purchase and loan eReaders for patrons to check out; should your library offer that option, that would give you some additional responsibility in this area for your own local choices. And, of course, eBooks can be read on computers within a library, so you may need to consider your options there also.

Many of the other technical pieces that need to be in place can be built by a library systems or supplied by library vendors. If you wish to control major portions of the system, you can contract with companies to provide individual parts. For example, you could contract with a vendor to provide the reading platform but provide all of the other pieces needed yourself. Or you could contract with a library eBook vendor to take care of all of parts for you. Discussion of the opportunities inherent in both methods follows in Chapter 3.

As you start planning for a new eBook collection, there are a number of key areas to keep in mind. This list identifies some of the main areas to watch for as you work with vendors, connect with patrons, or track developments and trends happening in this area.

Devices
- What types of devices are being used to read eBooks? Dedicated eReaders, or tablets and smartphones?
- What types and brands of dedicated eReaders are your patrons using?
- What types and brands of multipurpose devices are they using?
- Are patrons using multiple devices, or moving from one type of device to another?

Selecting, purchasing, and cataloging content
- What content is available for your patrons? What's available for free, or to purchase?
- Are there changes happening in the types of content that's available?
  - Is there more content being offered? Or more types of content?
  - Is there any content that is no longer available?
- How many purchasing models are being used by publishers?
- What is changing in terms of cataloging of eBook material?

Figure 2.1   Key Areas to Consider When Planning for a New eBook Collection

Reading experience, or types of platforms available
- What platforms are being used to read eBooks? Web based? Vendor apps?
- What operating systems are most prevalent? Are your patrons changing what they use?
- What is the reading experience for library patrons of library eBooks? Is the vendor website designed to be easy for your patrons to use?

Digital Rights Management and related protections
- What type of Digital Rights Management (DRM) is being used?
- Are there changes in the types of requirements for applying DRM?
- Is there content available without DRM?

What file types are most popular?
- Are your patrons using devices that use the industry standard file types (EPUB, etc.) or proprietary or vendor-specific file types?
- Are your patrons moving from devices that use one file type to another type of device?

Library-specific issues
- What methods are available to manage the library lending process?
- What is changing in terms of consortial or interlibrary loan lending for eBooks?
- What methods are available for patrons to manage their library experience? Are there wishlists, API integration options, or related areas of interest to your patrons?

Figure 2.1   (Continued)

CHAPTER 3

How Do Libraries Get eBooks?

You've heard from your patrons that they're interested in eBooks and you now have a general understanding of what's involved in offering eBooks. You've started talking with your stakeholders about what outcomes they are looking for with a launch of an eBook collection. You're determining how you'll fund and support a new or expanded service to meet your patron's demand for eBooks. With this knowledge, you're now ready to determine which method or methods you'd like to use to get eBooks into the hands, or devices, of your patrons.

In general, there are three main avenues for you to obtain eBooks: free eBooks, creating an eBook system yourself, and contracting with vendors. There are free eBooks on the Internet, and your staff can create pathways to direct your patrons to those resources. You could establish your own relationships with publishers, and develop your own eBook platform and services and host the books yourself. Or you can contract with a vendor to offer and host eBooks for your patrons, with the vendor managing the relationships with the publishers and other details. It's possible for you to implement and use all three of these models in your library at the same time. You can direct patrons to free books while managing your own platform and also purchasing a vendor service or services, and you can use the patron feedback you developed based on your work from Chapter 1 to determine how you want to approach your choices.

FREE ONLINE eBOOKS

A quick Internet search will net a variety of collections of free eBooks. One simple way of offering eBooks is to point your patrons from your website or catalog to these collections of free eBooks. This can be an easy way to get started with an eBook collection, since it doesn't require you to purchase any titles or develop any additional platforms. Many libraries direct patrons to these collections in addition to other vendor or publisher collections, since they provide unique access to titles that may not be available in other ways. However, there are some library eBook vendors who can make a curated collection of free eBooks available to your patrons if you so choose.

Some of these free eBooks are collections of books by beginning authors who are happy to have their works discoverable by library patrons. Other collections, like Project Gutenberg (http://www.gutenberg.org), focus on books in the public domain. However, Project Gutenberg is also soliciting current eBooks from self-published authors and small publishers, so their collection and scope continues to expand. From the Project Gutenberg site you will see other companies and organizations with whom it is collaborating. From that list of companies and affiliates you may find other collections of interest to your patrons. If you are on a hunt to find a multitude of free eBook collections, starting with a known and trusted site and looking at who they are featuring from their site is a great way to collect ideas. Then of course, you can evaluate each of the other collections to see if they fit with your scope of service.

Linking to free eBook collections can be an easy way to start your foray into offering eBooks, but one of its disadvantages is that most of these collections of eBooks span a wide variety of topics and types of books. Perhaps you had decided after looking at data that was mentioned in Chapter 1 and talking to your patrons, that you wanted to focus on a particular type of eBook: perhaps narrative nonfiction. These free eBook collections may include narrative nonfiction, but they most likely include a multitude of other topics as well. Measuring success is discussed in Chapter 6, but if you wanted to start with a limited collection in order to determine whether your patrons are interested in eBooks, offering only a broad site of free eBooks will make it more difficult to measure success. Therefore, many libraries direct patrons not only to these collections of free eBooks, but they also adopt another strategy. Sometimes libraries develop their own eBook system or contract with a library vendor and then purchase eBooks according to their service plan. And some libraries employ all three options: free eBooks, their own system, and vendor-based system(s).

DEVELOP AND MAINTAIN YOUR OWN SYSTEM

Another way to provide eBooks for your patrons is to create your own platform where you control all aspects of purchasing, hosting, and providing access to eBooks for your patrons. In this model, your library becomes the eBook provider. This can provide an opportunity for more local control and flexibility, but also requires the library to take on direct responsibility for more parts of the process. As mentioned in Chapter 2, there are a host of technical pieces that need to be in place in order to offer eBooks to library patrons. You need the content, the actual eBook files. This fact will be reiterated in other portions of this book as well, but one fact to keep in mind when thinking about purchasing eBooks directly from publishers: publishers do not have to sell eBooks to libraries. They do have to sell physical materials to you, based on the current U.S. copyright law, but eBooks are not included in the law. Selling eBooks to libraries is entirely up to the publisher's discretion. Even if you regularly buy print materials from a publisher, you may have a different experience when you attempt to purchase eBooks. This is also the case for library eBook vendors; there may be times when they aren't able to work with publishers or purchase materials because publishers have not made them available to libraries. To find the relevant sections on copyright, refer to 17 U.S.C. § 109: US Code—Section 109: Limitations on exclusive rights: Effect of transfer of particular copy or phonorecord (http://codes .lp.findlaw.com/uscode/17/1/109#sthash.C6iUQtfC.dpuf).

Some titles still have not been made available in an eBook version. Some titles might be considered standards or contemporary classics, but as of yet, they have no eBook version available. This is becoming increasingly rare for new titles, as publishers now consider physical and eBook versions as standard formats to be produced. These older titles without an eBook version are still under copyright, and the author or copyright holder has not permitted an eBook version to be published. The copyright holders could change their mind at any moment. If you are looking for a particular well-known title as an eBook and don't find for purchase, it is usually easy to verify with a publisher, online bookstore, or vendor that the title is currently unavailable.

In this model where you develop and maintain your own system, you or your staff work directly with publishers to purchase, or lease, eBook copies for the library. This can be one of the more complicated parts of the process, since you are setting out to purchase eBooks that you wish to lend out to patrons again and again and again. Some publishers will be excited to work with you, while other publishers as mentioned earlier may have no interest in selling to you at all. If you're managing the process yourself, you may not have vendor-provided selection tools like you would if you were working with a print or eBook vendor. You may need to develop your own process to track and coordinate title selection and budget information. In addition, you will probably need to be actively involved in contracting with publishers for access and licensing issues. Contracting with publishers is not something you need to do to purchase the vast majority of print materials for your collection. But being able to work directly with publishers, including small presses, is a great way to be responsive to local needs and highlight local resources. But it also comes with some additional requirements related to managing selection and purchasing that are aligned with, but different from, your print collections.

Once you have purchased the files, you need a number of other elements to be in place. For instance, you need a place for the files to live (servers), you need the lending mechanism that can manage the loaning of the eBook, the interface for your patrons to discover your eBooks, and the reading platform. Assuming you will be supporting a digital rights management (DRM) method and will have some sort of loan period for patrons to use and return or lose access to copies of the books, you will need to have the software to manage these processes for you. While there are a number of ways to approach the issue of rights and privacy, as well as loan periods, when you're working directly publishers and not using vendor tools, you'll still need the tools to manage access to your collection and to comply with any licensing or contractual requirements from the publishers.

Discovery and delivery are two other necessary components of your system. Discovery is the way patrons will find the books you have in your collection, and delivery is the means by which patrons will be able to download, or check out, titles from your collection. If you are developing your own system, you will need to determine the majority of the details related to these areas, or work with a vendor for some of the components you'll need.

If one of your discovery methods will be your library catalog, you will need to have a MARC record for each eBook. There are multiple options to obtain MARC records for your own eBooks. One method is have your own staff catalog the eBooks. Or if your library has a subscription to bibliographic database like Online Computer Library Center, Inc. (OCLC) and if the title is in the database, you can use MARC records already created by contributing members. Another option is to use publisher-supplied MARC records. Some of the publishers you work with may have MARC records available; these may be free, or there may be a fee for them. If you use publisher-supplied MARC records, you will want to review what you receive from the publishers to make sure they are what you need for your catalog, and you should be prepared to adjust them if they don't have all of the information you need. You will want to confirm that all of the fields needed for discovery in your system are in place, and that there aren't additional fields that need to be removed. You have to do due diligence to make sure that the eBook records are displaying correctly in your catalog, as each publisher you work with will have different expertise with MARC records. Determining what fields you need for your catalog and testing the records to see that they display the way you want them to in your catalog are steps you will need to take regardless of how you obtain MARC records.

In addition to adding the MARC records to your catalog to aid discovery, you may want to consider a separate web interface just for these materials. Just as we create separate shelving for different physical collections like mysteries and romances, one of the most current common discovery methods is to put all of the information on a separate eBook website so all of your eBooks can be found together. In addition, librarians are experimenting with a variety of ways to highlight their eBook collections, including setting up dedicated computers with some of them being set up using touch screens for patrons to browse collections. Some libraries project their website content in their buildings using digital signage technology, sometimes focusing on just their eBook content and sometimes integrating highlighting eBooks as well as other library services and collections.

Once your patrons have found what eBooks you have, the last part in the chain is delivery. You will need to address issues related to DRM, and determine how patrons will be able to get the eBooks from you. What file types will you support? You will need to know what your response will be to patrons who use primarily proprietary file types like Amazon's AZW. How will you address storage? Will you have a loan period model, where the access to the book will expire after a few weeks, or will patrons be able to retain a copy of the book? You'll need to build a process that lets patrons get the books from you onto their devices simply and easily.

Included in delivery is not only the method for a patron to obtain the eBook, but also the reading experience itself. This includes the way the digital file works on patrons' reading devices, and how well it will work for them once they get it from the library. How well does the digital file fit on a patron's reading device? Does the type flow from one page to another seamlessly? Can a patron change font size? Can a patron change font colors or have black font on a white background or vice versa? Can a patron add bookmarks? Will the bookmarks transfer across reading devices? Can patrons add their own notes or annotations? Your need to address some of these issues depending on the types of files you receive from the publishers. You should be prepared to determine the service and technical standards in this area should they be needed. As talked about in Chapter 2, with the rise of eBooks came expectations for a certain standard of ease of use. Functionality like bookmarking, bookmarking across multiple devices, changing font and style, and options for font color and backgrounds are now standard expectation for readers. If you are creating your own eBook platform, you need to provide as many of these "basic" requirements as possible.

If you are interested in the possibilities inherent in creating your own system but you don't not have all of the technical expertise on staff or all of the resources, the system can be broken down in parts and you can purchase or contract with companies to provide various pieces. For instance, there are companies who have built reading platforms and there are companies who provide servers and server management.

This model puts the library in charge of all of the components of developing and managing the entirety of the eBook service and gives you great flexibility to design a system that fits your needs. There are, however, many parts to the system. If you employ this option, you want to make sure you can support the system you've built now and also into the future as technology changes.

CONTRACTING WITH AN eBOOK VENDOR

Creating your own platform is possible, and as suggested, if you do not have the expertise in-house, there are companies available who can provide you with the pieces you need to manage your own system. Of course, the other option would be to contract with a vendor or vendors who can supply the entire system for your patrons: collection, hosting/storing the collection, discovery, and delivery. With all-in-one vendors, you do lose some of the ability to customize for your patrons, because vendors cannot be everything to every library system. But you also don't need to have the expertise or spend the time to maintain all of the components of the system yourself.

VENDOR SELECTION

Currently, there are a number of eBook vendors selling systems to libraries. Most of these are offering a complete platform: management of the publisher relationships, development of selection and budget management tools, discovery points and websites, MARC records and related cataloging, and delivery methods. As you start reviewing vendor options, we suggest you review all parts of the vendor's platform before moving ahead with a decision. There are vendors with great content and good publisher relationships, but their selection tools for staff and discovery and delivery methods for patrons may not be as seamless as you wish. And there are vendors with great patron websites but very limited content. Obviously you will be looking for a vendor to supply all of the pieces that you would need if you created your own platform to offer eBooks, and have them function at a high level. If a vendor has good content, but the overall experience for your patrons and staff will be difficult or confusing, you should definitely consider what this will mean for implementation. Likewise, if the patron experience is easy, but the content that your patrons are looking for is not there, your patrons are not likely to use the collection. Again, consider what this will be like as your patrons and staff start using this system. You want many things from a vendor. In fact, you need many things from a vendor, but first and foremost, you will look for content your patrons really want as well as an excellent patron experience.

The process you use to select a vendor or vendors will depend on the purchasing rules of your governing body. Many library systems use a request for purchase (RFP) or request for information (RFI) process to find an eBook vendor or vendors. With an RFP process you can describe exactly what you are looking for from an eBook vendor to best serve your patrons. You can also ask through this process for the ability to explore the vendor's product. Often the most useful part of the process is this ability to play with the product and evaluate it with your patrons in mind. Many library systems that have used an RFP process have posted their versions to the Internet so a search should quickly bring up other examples which you can use for ideas and questions to match your system's needs. A sample RFP and sample RFP evaluation tool are shown at the end of this chapter (Figures 3.1 and 3.2).

CONTENT SELECTION

What type of content are you looking for? Answering this question for yourself will give you the questions to ask potential vendors. For example, perhaps you are looking for a vendor or vendors to offer current content from major publishers for all age levels, both fiction and nonfiction. You can ask your potential vendors:

- How many and which publishers do they work with?
- How many current releases (this year) they have from each publisher?
- How many eBooks do they currently have available for purchase?
- How many eBooks are adult and how many are children's?
- How many fiction eBooks do they carry and how many nonfiction?
- For nonfiction, what subjects do they carry?

An expanded version of this checklist is found at the end of this chapter (Figure 3.2).

If you are starting with a specific need, you can tailor your questions. For example, perhaps your local school district has provided a tablet/reading device to every student and you wish to provide collection support to for grades K-6. You could use these questions but also ask about or look for specific publishers. Or even specific titles if you have reading lists from your school district. With this type of example, you can also describe to the vendors the type of service you want to provide, for example, eBook collection support for grades K-6. You can then ask, based on this description, what can you offer us? Vendors may surprise you with offerings and ideas you hadn't thought about and that you may wish to pursue.

AGE LEVELS AND SUBJECTS

In most cases, the age level and subject headings are usually assigned by the publisher, not the vendor. What you may have decided is a children's or teen title for your library may have been assigned a different age level by the publisher. Likewise, the publishers may assign subject headings or other categories that do not align with how you have cataloged the physical version of the title. What to do about this conflict is discussed in Chapters 4 and 5, but it's something you should be aware of when looking at vendor content, since it may lead to more work for your library as you expand your collection.

You can ask your potential vendors for a list of the publishers they work with. We have moved to a time where most publishers are working with most eBook vendors, which was not the case until fairly recently. You do want to check that publishers you expect to see on a vendor's list are there, and not just assume that all publishers are selling to all vendors. In addition, you'll want to review which vendors are carrying any of the smaller or local presses you know you'll be interested in. If you have local presses in your area, you may want to look for vendors who carry them, since your patrons will expect to see their books in your collection.

VENDOR-PROVIDED eBOOK FORMATS

As mentioned before, there are a number of eBook formats currently in use, including EPUB, EPUB3, and PDF, as well as some proprietary formats (e.g., AZW). As you start reviewing vendor options, you will need to consider what formats a vendor is able to offer. Like devices, eBook formats are changing frequently and are as important to monitor as changes to devices and reader behavior. Certain formats work better on some devices than others, so it is important to go back to what you learned from your patrons about what devices they will be using. For example, if you find your patrons are currently doing the majority of their reading on mobile devices, then you may want to look a vendor whose offerings are not primarily PDF. Vendors are doing whatever they can to make eBook devices agnostic, so they will work easily across a wide range of devices. A vendor's best business model is to have the eBooks it offers work on any device the patron is using. While that's increasingly the case, you'll want to make sure that the vendor you're reviewing is offering formats that your patrons can actually use.

VENDOR TOOLS FOR THE ACQUISITION OF eBOOKS

While the patron experience is of primary importance, the quality of the vendor tool used in acquisition is also important. Vendors can give you demos of their acquisition tools. You can also ask for a demo account so you can get a feel for the tool yourself.

Vendors want to help you spend money on collection so they will have "help" available from pre-selected lists to librarians on the vendor's staff who will create lists based on your specifications. Many vendors have best-seller lists based on national lists but also their own best-seller lists. Investigate everything that a vendor has to offer in terms of collection development; what do the vendors have that would be useful and make your selection easier?

The vendor's acquisition tool is usually the tool that provides performance information on your eBook collection. Since this will be how you are able to evaluate how your collection is performing, you'll want to understand how robust the tool is, and what it can do. Are all the circulation statistical reports you expect to have available included and easy to use? Some reports to look for include: number of titles owned, number of copies owned, circulation reports that can be run on specific date ranges, number of active users, number of patrons who have titles on hold, number of titles that have holds on them. What kinds of holds management reports are available? Whatever your hold to copy parameters, you want to be able to respond quickly when adding more copies. Most vendors have the ability to produce lists of titles that are above your hold to copy ratio and if you wish, the orders can be placed automatically. What reports does the vendor have available to report to you on the content you've purchased? You'll want to be able to find data on what's happening with specific parts of the eBook collection. If you are launching your eBook collection based on the type of information described in Chapter 1, see if the vendor's reports are robust enough to help you evaluate an eBook collection using some of those criteria. Publishers are using an increasingly wide number of purchasing models, from purchasing based on a limited number of checkouts to the length of time a library can have the file before it must repurchase the title. Check to see that the reports the vendor supplies will allow library staff to manage the publisher various models efficiently.

When evaluating the vendor's acquisition tool, look to see that all the searchable fields you want are included. You'll want to make sure that the access points they provide will be enough to meet the needs of your acquisitions staff.

Basic access points you'll want to check for should include:

- Title
- Author
- Publisher
- Publisher imprint
- ISBN
- Subject
- Original publication date of physical version
- eBook publication date
- Date of entry in vendor's database
- Other fields you may want to improve search or other access. Look to your other vendor tools to remind you of other expectations you have for searching for content

Once you've done a search within the vendor's tool, evaluate how the search results are returned to you. Just as patrons are looking for as few clicks as possible between them and the content they want, you and your staff are looking for the easiest, clearest ways of determining what to purchase with as few clicks as possible. For example, when running searches you may turn up results for content you've already purchased; is it easy to see this within the search results or do you have to do multiple clicks to find the information? Likewise, how easy is it to see what the purchasing terms are for each title? In other words, is it readily apparent that a title is perpetual access, or will you be purchasing a limited number of loans, or for a specific time period? You do not want this information hidden behind multiple clicks, since this will make it more difficult for you to manage your collections and budget.

Look at how you will order from the vendor. Most vendors are using a shopping cart-type process, similar to what's used with vendors of physical materials. Can the vendor's carts be assimilated easily into your overall ordering process? How will you transfer the cart information into your financial system? Again, the way this process works will potentially have an impact on the way library staff will be able to purchase materials, and how they will be able to track what is purchased. The more complicated this process is, or the larger the number of steps needed to align this with your other purchasing and budgeting tools, the more time it will take and the greater impact it will have on the overall efficiency and accuracy of your selection process.

Once you purchase eBooks from the vendor, you'll want to understand how long it will take for the eBooks to be available for your patrons to check out. You'll need to review the options the vendor has for billing and invoicing. If your institution or governing body has specific invoicing requirements, you'll also want to confirm that the vendor's procedure will work for what's needed by your organization. And you'll also want to make sure you understand and can explain how long it will take from when you make the purchase to when the title becomes available for your patrons. Since the goal is to get the eBooks out to readers as soon as possible, especially if you are purchasing with a model that is tied to a time limit for use, maximizing the availability of the title is important. Knowing what's needed to move from selecting the title, through the library's invoicing and purchasing channels, to the vendor, and then back to the library for your patrons to use will be an important part of your vendor review process.

MARC RECORDS

Before looking at the options for obtaining MARC records for eBooks, you'll need to decide whether you would like eBooks discoverable within your library catalog or not. Your eBook collection will be discoverable on the unique website the vendor builds for your library regardless of your decision. But adding MARC records to your catalog does signal to your patrons that eBooks are part of the entire collection. eBooks are another format option you are making available for your patrons to choose from.

When you submit an order to a vendor, often you will receive brief bibliographic information in return. This information can be reformatted as a brief MARC record and added to your catalog. The information will include basic information for each item, including the title, author, publisher, publication date, and the link to the eBook file on the vendor site. There will be no access by subject in the brief record, but this small record may be enough for your purpose.

eBook vendors usually have full MARC records available for purchase from affiliate vendors. The eBook vendor will send to the affiliate vendor lists of what you have ordered from them and then the affiliate will send you a complete record once the eBook has been cataloged. You can ask for sample MARC records from the affiliates to evaluate how they will work within your catalog. As you implement MARC records in your library's catalog, you'll want to review how they align with the rest of the MARC records in your catalog, and which option is best for the types of materials you're purchasing. If you're purchasing mostly popular fiction or similar materials, the brief MARC record with no subject access may work for your patrons. If you are purchasing heavily in nonfiction, having subject access in your catalog may be important for your patrons to be able to find those materials. Both the brief and complete MARC records are good options, and it's possible to start with one type and move to the other as your collection expands or your patrons become more familiar with using your catalog and not solely the vendor site to find eBooks.

API AVAILABILITY

Many libraries use an application programming interface, or API, to integrate vendor information about collections and availability directly into their catalog or other online services. An increasing number of eBook and ILS vendors are supplying the code, the routines, the protocols, or an API so that you can have disparate proprietary systems talk to each other's system. Using an API, you pull pieces of information from one system into the other's system.

For example, implementing an API can allow you to offer patrons the ability to view eBook availability (i.e., is the eBook available for checkout right now?) right from your catalog even though the eBook is still being managed by your eBook vendor. Patrons could also manage their accounts directly in the library catalog with their other materials, instead of needing to use the vendor website. Many vendors are now providing this type of access, and it can be a great way to improve service for library patrons by reducing the number of clicks they need to do to get to the information they want to see.

When looking into the vendor's API, you'll want to clearly identify what types of information you'll want to have access to about collection items and availability. In general, you'll want to make sure the API will provide the current number of copies owned, the number of copies available for checkout, and holds within the bibliographic record in your catalog, as well as information that patrons would expect to see as part of their library experience. Information like number of eBooks the patrons has checked out, titles on hold, and what place is the patron in the holds queue. These data points are almost standard now in an API, and these points will allow you to provide titles and availability in your own catalog, as well as allow patrons to see their account information, depending on how the API is integrated into your catalog. Other information may be available as well, and you'll want to watch to see what other data points are being developed. New data points may give you valuable new services to offer your patrons.

COMPATIBILITY WITH YOUR INTEGRATED LIBRARY SYSTEM (ILS)

If you are planning to provide other functionality, like an API, in your catalog, you'll need to ensure that your eBook vendor is compatible or working with your ILS vendor. This is yet another example of the complexity of the eBook system that was discussed in Chapter 2. Integrating information and functionality between your ILS vendor and your eBook vendor means that the two companies have to be willing to work on software that works for both parties. Luckily, this is a time where ILS vendors and library eBook vendors are willing to work together to expand functionality that benefits our patrons. The more benefits to your patrons, the more that libraries are likely to sustain and/or expand service. You will want to confirm that the eBook vendor or vendors that you are considering do indeed have partnerships with your ILS vendors. And you will want to discover exactly what functionality they can provide. Look for the data points just mentioned: the current number of copies owned, the number of copies available for checkout, and holds within the bibliographic record in your catalog, as well as patron account information. Common information includes number of eBooks the patrons has checked out, titles on hold, and hold queue information.

RESTRICTING ACCESS TO YOUR eBOOK COLLECTION

Many libraries have limits on who can check out eBooks. These types of limits may be linked to fine and fees or other library policies, they may be set by geographic boundaries or type of cardholder, or there may be other types of restrictions that need to be accommodated. These types of restrictions are fairly common with physical materials, and you and your staff and patrons are already familiar with how they work and how they are implemented.

eBooks may provide some new things to consider in this area, especially if other libraries in your area are not providing eBooks, or if your collection differs significantly from what is available in nearby areas. This is especially true since library patrons don't need to come into your library to access your eBooks. Geographical boundaries are less relevant to potential users of online content. They are focusing more on access and their experience with other online content, which may be more freely available. Those patrons may ask why there are limitations on who can access your eBook collection, or why the limits are the same (or different) from what's in place with your other collections. You may also find you are connecting with new users who aren't familiar with any restrictions in place for your physical items. New users may need explanations about why a library may need to restrict access.

As you implement your eBook collection, you'll want to evaluate and question any of the restrictions you currently have and determine if they are going to be applied to eBook patrons. If you limit circulation of print books to users who live or work in a specific geographic area, does this need to be the case for your eBook collection also? The answer may be yes, because this type of restriction may be tied to the way your library is structured and/or funded. Or a restriction may come as part of your contract with your vendors. But perhaps you don't need to restrict eBook access. If so, you need to decide if you would like to have access to your eBook collection operate with different rules than your physical collection. Whether you restrict access or not may not be an area where you have much flexibility. Regardless of the decisions you make or have to make, you should be prepared to speak to the question of access as you add a new format to your collection.

Even if you don't need or want to restrict access based on vendor specifications or library structure, many libraries limit access to physical materials to patrons who owe fines or other fees, since they often come from late or lost materials. Will those limitations carry over to their eBook use also? Some libraries decide to treat access to all "books" the same way; if a patron has fines over a certain level, he or she loses access to checking out books, regardless of formats. Other libraries approach eBooks as an online resource; fines are related to physical materials, but don't impact access to databases and, by extension, eBooks and other downloadable content. Both of these options may be successful for your library, but they do represent distinct approaches to how you consider your eBook collection working with the rest of your collections, and how you'll be framing decisions about access as your collection expands.

If your library or library system needs to limit circulation in some way, you will need to confirm that the vendor is able to support your requirements, and that its solution is compatible with your ILS. Working through some of these questions as you plan to launch your collection will make sure your library staff are prepared to work with potential vendors on access and setup issues, as well as to work with patrons as they begin to use the new collection.

COMPATIBILITY WITH PATRON DEVICES

The devices patrons use to read eBooks continue to change. While this is a continually evolving part of the current environment, you need to look what information you have as to what devices your patrons are using with their eBooks. You may be able to use the patron feedback collected through a process like the one we suggested in Chapter 1, or you may have actual use data from your patrons. As you work with vendors, you'll want to confirm that their tools work with the devices that are actually being used in your community.

When you start evaluating and comparing vendors as part of your RFP, RFI, or contracting process, take the time to try out the vendor's product on the actual devices your patrons are using. You want to see for yourself what steps your patrons will have to go through in order to check out and read eBooks from your collection, and confirm that you'll have access to all of the other functionalities you expect. Is the process as easy as the vendor is advertising? Or are there extra clicks or actions you weren't expecting that will slow down or frustrate your patrons? If possible, it's worth having a variety of people with different technical skills walk through the process and then compare their experiences.

VENDOR WEBSITE FOR YOUR LIBRARY

While many libraries include or integrate eBook collections into their catalogs, the vendor websites also play a key role in the delivery of your eBook service. Patrons may use the vendor website to select titles, check them out and return them, download any required software, or get other assistance. In many cases, the vendor website may be the only way your patrons access your collection, so you'll want to make sure that using that website is easy and can be aligned with your needs.

In general, you'll want to make sure that the vendor will allow you to customize the "catalog" on its website, so you'll be able to organize or group the books in your collection in ways that are meaningful to your patrons and that align with how you're presenting your print collection. You may want to be able to include your logo and have the colors and general design align with your library website or other marketing needs. And you'll also want to make sure that you should be able to link easily to their site, and that patrons using their site are able to get back to your site. You want to make sure your patrons have a seamless experience, especially for many of them this may become one of the main ways they connect with the library.

WHAT IS AVAILABLE ON THE VENDOR SITE?

For many of your patrons, the vendor's site will be the primary way they search for, check out, and return library eBooks. At a minimum, your patrons will expect it to work the same way as your catalog works for their physical books, with the same functions and options. If your patrons purchase eBooks or other materials online, they may also expect your eBook collection to have some of the same features and functionality that they're used to in these other environments. As you review what's available from vendors, you'll want to remember that your patrons are bringing their own expectations about how this online experience should work for them.

One of the first areas you'll want to consider is the mix of options the vendor provides for managing patron requests and checkouts. Your patrons will be using this site to place reserves and manage their accounts, so this part of the vendor site needs to work smoothly and be easy to use. You'll want to evaluate the process for checking out a book from the start of the process to when the item is returned. This will include the steps for placing a hold on a book, suspending a hold, and canceling a hold that's no longer wanted. Patrons will expect to be able to return an eBook when they're done with it and not wait until the loan period expires, so you'll want to understand how this functionality will work for your patrons. Renewing titles is something patrons are used to being able to do with physical books, but isn't always available with eBooks, and if it is, it may not work the same way that they're used to. You'll also want to review how patrons are notified about their eBooks when they become available. The vendor usually sends an e-mail to the patron; you should be able to customize the text and branding at a basic level so your patrons will recognize that the message is from their library, and that it's an eBook, not a physical item.

In addition to the regular request process, your patrons probably expect to be able to have a "wishlist" or other ways to track books they'd like to read at some point in the future. This is especially true if you have a circulation limit or other restrictions that will impact how many books a patron can check out at a time. Tracking titles with a wishlist is functionality that your patrons will probably expect as wishlist or saved lists are available from many online retailers. How the vendor's wishlist works for patrons is an important part of your patron's experience with your collection. Reviewing all of these components will help you determine if the vendor website will meet your needs, and will also give you a preliminary understanding of how much staff and patron training and support may be needed as you move ahead with this service.

In addition to this standard functionality, vendor websites now often include expanded information about the items in the collection. This can include descriptive information about the book, cover art, professional reviews, sample text, and other content that helps the reader learn more about the book. You have a number of expectations as to what you should see when you look up a title in an online catalog. If you are trying out a vendor product and don't see cover images, for example, the product will probably feel incomplete or unfinished. Think about what other expectations you have when you are looking up a title. You probably expect to see a description or brief summary of the book. But are you also expecting to see reviews if they exist? If so, from which review sources? Journals? Newspapers? Or perhaps reader websites that offer reviews or ratings? Do you also want to include places where the readers can review and rate the books themselves and contribute to the overall experience?

Librarians specialize in creating excellent metadata, for instance, authorizing author names so that you can find all of an author's works in one search regardless of variations. Try out some author searches in the vendor site to see if what you are expecting turns up in the search. Much of the title, author, and description information is being given to the vendor by the publisher, but if the information provided doesn't give the patron what he or she expects, it is going to be frustrating for the patron.

All of these features can vary by vendor, and you'll want to explore what's possible as you compare vendor sites. What type of content are you looking for? If you have some of this functionality integrated into your catalog for your physical collection, do you want at a minimum the same information available for your eBook collection? Knowing your answers to these questions will give you the questions to ask potential vendors.

OTHER VENDOR SERVICES

Most publishers are now trying to work with as many eBook vendors as possible. As the content becomes less distinct between vendors, their services and how they deliver them are what separate vendors from each other. Explore each vendor's product in terms of services offered to see what new opportunities may be available. For example, some vendors offer standalone kiosks where patrons can explore and check out eBooks. Or perhaps your library is interested in a "buy it now" functionality. If so, some vendors can provide that for your library system. Also, take advantage of vendor sales calls or webinars to find out what's in development from the vendors. If you are using an RFI process and you are having vendors prepare presentations for you, be watching for other services that the vendor has available. These may be services you hadn't thought of but may fit into your service plan or are intriguing as future options.

WHAT DOES IT TAKE TO LAUNCH THE PRODUCT?

Whether you have no dedicated technical staff or a number of people on staff who are dedicated to library IT support, look into what is needed to launch the vendor's product. Once again, this is where it is beneficial to have a cross-functional team to be a part of your planning process. As you consider vendor products, you'll want to make sure you have a full understanding of what it would take to launch the site. Discuss with your staff or team and the vendor as to what tasks you will need to take on, and what's provided by the vendor within your contract. As you review your options in this area, you can ask for a sample implementation plan. As you are evaluating vendors, you can compare vendor requirements for launching the product. Vendors should be able to provide you with fairly extensive documentation on the launch process, including the roles and responsibilities for each partner. You'll want to make sure that your library has the capacity to do what is needed as you determine if this is the right path for your library.

Any vendor should be able to answer all of the questions we covered earlier through a questionnaire or product demo. Even if you pursue those options, you should also take the time to try the product yourself and get some hands-on experience with it. If possible, have a number of different people try the product with the goal of answering all of the questions you consider to be most important. If you can pull together a group with different strengths and interests, you will gain valuable insights into how the product may work for your staff and patrons.

Of course, selecting a vendor product with the best functionality is only part of the process. Once you select a product that interests you, you'll need to consider the overall cost of using the platform. There are generally two areas that the vendor charges for: the initial start-up fee for the use of its platform and an annual maintenance fee. The initial start-up costs will need to be factored into your planning for funding your collection launch, since this is an important part of getting your system up and running. In addition to this "membership" fee, your collection will be a separate expense on a title-by-title basis. Managing collection costs will be covered in Chapter 4.

With all of these factors to consider, it may feel like choosing an eBook vendor is a terribly complicated process. But by sorting out which questions are most important to your patrons, and knowing what capacity you have to implement, you can streamline both the process and your decision making. Earlier in the chapter, we advocated for both excellent content and an excellent patron experience as the two most critical parts of your decision. As you work through this process, you'll develop a better understanding of how that balance will work for your library, and can bring that knowledge forward into your new collection.

CONCLUSION

No-one-size-fits all solution is available to offering eBooks. Three models were described: free eBooks, creating your own system, and contracting with a library eBook vendor all have both positives and limitations. Free eBooks, especially when linking to other sites, are indeed free, but if you are seeking to give your patrons a focused collection, free eBooks are almost impossible to curate. Building your own system gives you ultimate control and the ability to shape a system to exactly fit your patron needs. But there are many parts that need to be managed and you need to have the resources available to build and keep track of it all. In addition, if you are looking for particular content, you will have to work with publishers individually and they may or may not be interested in working with you. A library vendor may seem to be the best of both worlds. For instance, you can curate the content since you are selecting the titles, but because vendors need to make their product attractive to as many libraries as possible, you often lose the ability to set up the product to best suit your patrons. Since there is no one perfect solution to offering eBooks, many library systems implement more than one of these choices. Free eBooks plus a vendor product. Or multiple vendor products. Or all three models.

If you are just beginning with eBooks, we suggest picking the model that best suits your needs. If successful, you can always add on another model. Regardless of which model or models you choose, to us the most important overall considerations are to find the best possible content combined with the best possible patron experience.

This sample is intended as a way to get you started on an RFP process. It is in no means an exhaustive list of requirements, nor does it need to include every element we mention. Doing a web search should also bring you several other sample eBook vendor requirements. You should feel free to only add the elements that work best for your situation, and not ask for information you're not going to use.

Introduction
Library or library system description: a brief description of your library or library system. Where you're located, geographic information (e.g., urban, suburban, mix), number of branches if applicable, size of your service population, possibly demographics if you think it would be helpful to vendors bidding.

If you know you have a specific aim for your eBook collection, you can add it in this section. You'll most likely go into more detail later in the RFP, but it's helpful to briefly note it here as well. For example, if you were looking for a vendor and wanted to focus only on children's materials, you'd probably want to call it out early in the RFP, so vendors don't miss this important criterion.

Sample requirements
Devices
Library patrons should have the capability to download and/or access content on a variety of devices, including personal computers (e.g., Apple, PC, Android), laptops, MP3 players, tablets, dedicated eReaders/tablets (e.g., Kindle, Nook), and smartphones.

App availability
eBook vendors must be able to optimize library patron's mobile experience. Mobile apps must be available for Android, iOS, and Microsoft operating systems.

APIs
Vendor must supply APIs to permit ILS integration with ______________ (insert your ILS vendor name). Vendor-supplied APIs must display, at a minimum, current number of owned copies, available copies, and holds within the item catalog record and also list titles checked out, titles on hold, and place in wait queue in patron record. Vendor will provide technical support to implement APIs.

Website access
The downloadable media online service would be made available through a direct hyperlink from the library's website to the actual service provided by the vendor. Vendor should also make available applications (apps), hyperlinks to imbed in MARC (Machine Readable Cataloging) records, and other access points as available.

Support for the service
The downloadable media online service must be provided in real-time and available seven (7) days a week, twenty-four (24) hours a day. The library shall be notified of planned downtime for service/maintenance at least forty-eight (48) hours in advance of the planned downtime. If the downtime is unexpected due to equipment failure or other unforeseen circumstances, the library shall be notified within two (2) hours of the loss of service and within another two (2) hours receive notification as to the expected length of the downtime and the circumstances leading to the downtime.

Vendor must offer direct technical support to patrons and staff from__to__by telephone, chat, e-mail, or support form. If live access to technical support is not available, vendor must give response to message within 24 hours.

Figure 3.1 Sample Request for Proposal (RFP)

Scheduled maintenance preventing patron access to eBooks and platform must be performed at times and on days of lowest usage as monitored by vendor.

eBook acquisition

Vendors must have a robust acquisition system for the selection and maintenance of eBook collections.

If provided by publisher, vendor must list access titles' original publication date in database.

Vendor must provide library staff the ability to filter a vendor's database by "already purchased" and "not yet purchased."

Vendor must provide access to collection maintenance reports that provide historic and current data including titles in collection, number of copies, type of licensing, format, total holds placed on titles, holds on title for specific time period, current titles on hold, holds to title ratios, total circulation on title, circulation on title during specific time period.

Vendor must supply in a single report a list of current titles with holds, holds to title ratio, cost per copy, and current number of copies in collection to facilitate additional copy ordering.

All reports must be viewable within an Internet browser and downloadable to Microsoft Excel.

Content must be available within 48 hours of placing an order.

Vendors must provide either MARC records or metadata based on the eBook orders submitted. Metadata based on orders submited must be provided in Microsoft Excel spreadsheet form. MARC records need to be "delivered" to library within 48 hours after an order has been placed.

The vendor must provide an electronic catalog via vendor website of all titles available in their e-content services. The catalog should be searchable at a minimum by:

    a. Title
    b. Author
    c. Publisher
    d. ISBN/EAN/UPC or other standard inventory number
    e. Subject
    f. Publication date

Patron limits

Your library eBook collection is for use by _______(describe your restrictions; i.e., only your library patrons with a valid library card number will be able to check out eBooks).

Vendor must authenticate patrons using _______(this is the authentication protocol used by your library).

Vendor must allow _______to set circulation duration, circulation limits, renewal limits, hold request limits, and response period to hold notification for our patrons.

Patron experience

Vendor must supply patrons the means via the vendor's platform the option to place, cancel, and suspend holds on all titles that are not unlimited in use.

Vendor must supply "wishlist" capability for patrons.

Vendor must allow patrons the ability to bookmark across multiple devices.

Vendor must give patrons the ability to access content on and off line.

Vendor's eBook interface must contain functionality that allows patrons to change font, size, and layout of eBook content.

Vendor's platform must provide patrons the ability to "return" eBooks early if they wish.

Figure 3.1 (Continued)

Vendor must notify patrons of available holds via e-mail. Vendor must provide patrons the ability to change e-mail address for a specific title hold request without losing place in queue.

Vendor's catalog shall provide library patrons information about the titles available that includes, but limited to, a brief description or summary, publisher reviews, author information, and other similar information when available. Library patrons shall be able to navigate through an eBook to locate a specific page and/or chapter.

Title information shall indicate if the title is available and if there is a waiting list. Waiting list should indicate the number of patrons on list.

Customization

Library must have the ability to customize the electronic catalog on the vendor website. Customization should include adding logo and being able to match colors and general design of library's website. Vendor's website should also be able to link back to library's website.

Other information to request from vendor

The vendor shall provide the library its licensing agreement for e-content service with its proposal.

Vendor shall provide its data privacy policy which will describe what information is kept on patrons, the duration the information is kept and for what purpose.

Vendor must provide the list of devices that are compatible with its service.

The vendor shall provide the library with a list of publishers and suppliers used in providing the e-services content and total number of titles available by format. The list must include any restrictions on circulation and usage imposed by the publisher and/or supplier.

The vendor shall list whether there will be additional software, hardware, and/or platform support that the library should purchase in order to use the e-content services. The vendor shall list all the technical requirements involved in the use of such software, hardware, and/or platform support.

If there will be additional, hardware, and/or platform/hosting support, the vendor should list the start-up fees and related services fees.

The vendor must list if there is an additional charge for technical support in to the annual maintenance fee. If there is an additional charge, the vendor should list the charge per hour.

Implementation support

The vendor shall provide technical setup assistance by providing the library appropriate URL addresses and/or IP addresses.

The vendor shall provide training for the library's staff prior to going "live" either on-site or via video-conference training. If there is an additional charge for this, the related cost must be listed. Please explain how the training is conducted (on-site, video-conference, etc.).

The vendor shall provide online help content and FAQs for library customers accessing the content. Online help should be updated monthly and/or whenever new formats or features are added. The library should be provided a way to submit comments and/or suggestions for online help and FAQs.

Vendor shall indicate if library retains ownership of purchased titles regardless of if the library maintains the service. If the library chooses to terminate or not renew the contract, vendor should indicate how the digital files will be provided to the library and what formats will be used.

Terms

The term of this contract will be for _______. This contract shall include the purchase of downloadable media platforms and all services described in these specifications.

Figure 3.1   (Continued)

For the purposes of this contract, the online service is defined as downloadable and shared eBook titles. These titles are made available through the vendor's web-based services. The key functionality of this online service is to allow library users to browse, check out/download, and preview digital content.

Ordering methods
Vendor must accept purchase orders via ______________.

Invoicing
Vendor must provide invoices: (paper, electronic, other specifications)
    Items shall be arranged by library purchase order, and in title order within each purchase order.
    Purchase order number shall be shown on all invoices and related correspondences.

Qualifications
In order to be considered for award, vendors shall supply reference and contact information from at least three (3) public libraries that are using the vendor's services, and that serve more than _______ people and have more than _______ locations. (You may want references from libraries or systems similar to your own.)
    Vendors should have been in the business of supplying e-content for a minimum of two years.

Figure 3.1 (Continued)

Evaluator Name: _________________________________

Circle One:
Initial Evaluation
Reevaluation after Discussions
Post Interview (if applicable)

RATING TABLE

Excellent	Outstanding level of quality; significantly exceeds in all respects the minimum requirements; high probability of success; no significant weaknesses.
Very Good	Substantial response; meets in all aspects and, in some cases exceeds, the minimum requirements; good probability of success; no significant weaknesses.
Good	Generally meets minimum requirements; probability of success; weaknesses are minor and can be readily corrected.
Marginal	Lack of essential information; low probability for success; significant weaknesses, but correctable.
Unsatisfactory	Fails to meet minimum requirements; little likelihood of success; needs major revision to make it acceptable.

Figure 3.2 Individual Evaluator Worksheet

EVALUATION FACTORS

Evaluation Factor #1: Capabilities, features, and qualities of Proposer's eBook Content Services
- Strengths:
- Weaknesses:
- Deficiencies
- Qualitative Rating for This Evaluation Factor: _______________________________________

(Excellent, Very Good, Good, Marginal, or Unsatisfactory)

Evaluation Factor #2: Ease of patron experience
- Strengths:
- Weaknesses:
- Deficiencies
- Qualitative Rating for This Evaluation Factor: _______________________________________

(Excellent, Very Good, Good, Marginal, or Unsatisfactory)

Evaluation Factor #3: Proposer's relationships with publishers, including any exclusive relationships with publishers
- Strengths:
- Weaknesses:
- Deficiencies
- Qualitative Rating for This Evaluation Factor: _______________________________________

(Excellent, Very Good, Good, Marginal, or Unsatisfactory)

Evaluation Factor #4: Proposer's legal terms and proposed method to transfer titles upon termination
- Strengths:
- Weaknesses:
- Deficiencies
- Qualitative Rating for This Evaluation Factor: _______________________________________

(Excellent, Very Good, Good, Marginal, or Unsatisfactory)

Evaluation Factor #5: Proposer's number of titles
- Strengths:
- Weaknesses:
- Deficiencies
- Qualitative Rating for This Evaluation Factor: _______________________________________

(Excellent, Very Good, Good, Marginal, or Unsatisfactory)

Evaluation Factor #6: Proposer's cost
- Strengths:
- Weaknesses:
- Deficiencies
- Qualitative Rating for This Evaluation Factor: _______________________________________

(Excellent, Very Good, Good, Marginal, or Unsatisfactory)

Figure 3.2   (Continued)

Evaluation Factor #7: Proposer's number of eOriginals and the publishers supplying the originals
- Strengths:
- Weaknesses:
- Deficiencies
- Qualitative Rating for This Evaluation Factor: _______________________________________
                           (Excellent, Very Good, Good, Marginal, or Unsatisfactory)

Evaluation Factor #8: Proposer's past performance
- Strengths:
- Weaknesses:
- Deficiencies
- Qualitative Rating for This Evaluation Factor: _______________________________________
                           (Excellent, Very Good, Good, Marginal, or Unsatisfactory)

Evaluation Factor #9: Proposer's telephone or in-person interview, if requested
- Strengths:
- Weaknesses:
- Deficiencies
- Qualitative Rating for This Evaluation Factor: _______________________________________
                           (Excellent, Very Good, Good, Marginal, or Unsatisfactory)

INDIVIDUAL EVALUATOR SUMMARY

Summary Evaluation Rating: ____
               (Excellent, Very Good, Good, Marginal, or Unsatisfactory)

Apply the following scoring to prepare summary evaluation rating:
    Excellent: 4 points
    Very Good: 3 points
    Good: 2 points
    Marginal: 1 point
    Unsatisfactory: 0 points

Take average of points scored for each question. Use the average as a guide for your summary evaluation rating. Provide an explanation if your summary evaluation rating is unclear from a straight average of the ratings (e.g., if one criteria more heavily weighted than another)

Narrative Justification of Rating (Summarize strengths, weaknesses, and deficiencies):

Evaluator Signature
Date

Figure 3.2   (Continued)

As you start looking for vendors, or consider doing a Request for Proposal (RFP) you'll want to prepare a list of questions or criteria to use to evaluate your options. While the level of detail you'll need will vary by what's most important for your patrons and staff, you'll want to make sure you ask a wide range of questions to make sure you fully understand your options.

Collection questions
- How many publishers does the vendor work with?
- How many current releases (this year) they have from each publisher?
- How many eBooks do they currently have available for purchase?
- How many eBooks are adult, and how many are children's or teen?
- How many fiction eBooks do they carry and how many nonfiction?
- For fiction, what genres do they carry, and how many titles are in each category?
- For nonfiction, what subjects do they carry, and how many titles are in each category?

Circulation and access questions
- How easy is it for a patron to place a hold?
- How easy is it for a patron to cancel a hold?
- How easy is it for a patron to check out a title?
- Can a patron return an eBook before the loan period expires? If so, how easy is the process?
- Can the patron suspend holds?
- How is a patron notified that his or her eBook is available?
- Does the vendor have a "wishlist" capability so patrons can track titles they are interested in but not yet ready to place a hold on or check out?

Customer support
- How are library staff able to contact the vendor with patron questions (file-type issues, library card issues, etc.)?
- Are patrons able to contact the vendor with questions? How does this process work?
- What is the estimated response time for resolving patron questions?
- Does the vendor provide online help on their website? On their app? Is this information helpful and relevant for your patrons?

Other questions
- What other services is the vendor advertising?
- Is there a process patrons can use to suggest a title?

Figure 3.3 Sample Vendor Checklist

CHAPTER 4

Implementing a Vendor-Based eBook Collection

As discussed in Chapter 3, there are several ways that libraries are providing their patrons with access to eBooks. They are directing patrons to freely available eBooks on the Internet, working directly with publishers to obtain eBooks, working with vendor-provided collections and platforms, or any combination of those models. Currently, working with vendors for collections and access is the primary way that librarians are approaching this choice, even if they are also using the other methods. Since so many librarians are working with vendors to provide their primary access to eBooks, a full chapter is dedicated to this process.

FINDING THE MONEY

Assume that your library has determined to work with a vendor to provide a platform for your patrons to circulate its eBooks and for you and your staff to select and manage materials. You will need to start working on allocating the necessary funding and other resources to support this plan.

Determining the composition of your "opening day" eBook collection is one of your first steps on this path. You may have a good idea of what you want based on the pre-work you did in connecting with your patrons, since the feedback they provided may have set some clear direction for where they'd like you to start. But do you want to begin with a small collection and build steadily, or do you want to launch with hundreds or thousands of titles, knowing your collection may have to grow more slowly after that? Both options have their advantages and disadvantages for your patrons and your staff. A small collection allows you to learn from your patrons; you can monitor their holds and requests and respond accordingly as you learn more about what they're looking for. A large collection allows you to have more of a "wow" factor for your patrons right off the bat, giving them more titles and copies to choose from, and limiting the time they might need to wait for the books they want to read.

Building an eBook collection for a library has some interesting and perhaps unexpected collection management aspects. Unlike physical books, where the pricing is relatively the same regardless of publisher, eBook pricing varies by publisher, and sometimes the same publisher may have several pricing options. There is no agreement or standard practice on eBook pricing models for libraries as of yet. And with eBooks the price for access is only one part of the equation. How long you as a library can "keep" the eBook, or rather have access to it, varies by publisher as well. Purchasing an eBook for your library doesn't always mean that your patrons will have perpetual access to that title; you may actually only be leasing access to that title for a set amount of time or number of uses.

For the first time you not only have to track what titles you want, but also how long you can have access to the titles since you may not get to "keep" them. Then you make the decision about whether they are worth the price the publisher is charging for the title. Out of every four titles you purchase of a similar "type," you might have four different prices or might have access to the titles for several different lengths of time. Currently there is a publisher charging three times the average marketplace price, but a library then has permanent or perpetual access to the title. Another publisher is currently charging a price similar to the retail price of a physical book, but your library will be able to circulate the book only 26 times before access is removed and the book would need to be re-purchased. Another publisher's eBook titles need to be re-purchased on a yearly basis, and yet another publisher has a two-year lease model. There is also a cost per circulation model, where you have access to all of collection of titles and only pay when a patron checks a title out of the collection. Some publishers offer a simultaneous use model which works more like a database fee. The library pays for access like a database, and there is no limit as to how many patrons access the titles at the same time. In the consumer marketplace there is also the subscription model, where a customer pays a fee on an ongoing basis and then can have access to all within the database.

There are new models entering the library market and consumer market constantly. Some of the consumer models come into the library market, some do not. Some models seem to have staying power; some disappear after a short amount of time. But because there are currently such a variety of models being used, it is complicated to manage even a few of them. Each of the library models needs to be managed and their expenses planned for in your budget, and there's no guarantee that the models you're budgeting for this year will be available for you to use next year.

The necessary management of these various models can have significant implications for your selection and budgeting process, and can be especially problematic if you have obtained only one-time funding. One-time funding is wonderful to get you started, but even if you are entering eBooks as a pilot project, some of the titles you purchased may need to be re-purchased soon after you launch your collection, for example, the titles with a limited numbers of loans. Because of these repurchasing models, your one-time funding can be expended very quickly as you work to maintain access to the titles you already have let alone add any new titles to your collection.

If you are starting with one-time funding in this world of multiple purchasing models, you'll want to plan in advance how you will allocate your funding to minimize the chance of any unexpected funding shortages. You may want to divide your funding into these general categories:

- Percentage of budget allocated for first-time purchases of titles
- Percentage of budget allocated for repurchasing of titles that have expired because you have reached your allocated circulation limits or time periods
- Percentage of budget allocated to respond to patron requests and to purchase additional "copies" of eBooks of those titles your patrons are really interested in

BUDGETING

Assuming you are planning to make a long-term commitment to eBooks, how do you find money for them within your collection budget? Whether you have one-time start-up funding or will need to allocate funds from your general collection budget, you will need to consider how to approach the overall funding for your eBook collection. One way to start is to go back to the data you gathered in your environmental scan as you started planning your process. Are there some readers you know (or suspect) who would appreciate an eBook version rather than a physical version? Romance, science-fiction, and fantasy readers have been cited as preferring eBooks to physical versions. See http://io9 .com/why-science-fiction-is-where-the-action-is-for-e-books-587483766 and http://www .theguardian.com/books/2011/oct/10/romantic-fiction-eBooks as examples of reader preference changing. If you can verify that your romance, science-fiction, and fantasy patrons may prefer eBooks to physical versions, perhaps you can move some of your money from your print collection to eBooks. Transferring some of your funding will allow you to provide the same access to those collections but in different formats. Are there other formats that you would really like to stop buying, based on declining patron use? Perhaps part of your planning to start an eBook collection will give you the impetus to make that kind of change. For instance, you might like to reduce or completely stop purchasing some print reference materials and rely on solely on the electronic database versions of those titles, but have not had the push to actually implement a change in that area. The desire to begin offering eBooks can help you not only make the decision but give you the justification for change with some patrons or other stakeholders who might not be happy with the move. While it's never an easy process to stop purchasing a collection, being able to use those resources to help support a new collection or expand a service may help with the transition.

Likewise, there may be other collections that need attention and where your spending has been on auto-pilot. For example, maybe your library has added a service that provides online access to periodicals. If so, are there any changes you can make in your physical periodical budget? That might be a budget to consider adjusting to support the creation of an eBook collection. There are also video and music services available for libraries. Have you subscribed to any of those services and if so, have you already looked at the corresponding budgets for the physical versions? Even posing these questions, we acknowledge that these are seldom easy decisions and are often made within already-tight budgets. While you may be constantly asked to add the next new format (like eBooks), you are seldom if ever being asked to get rid of a format. Even low-use formats and collections have users and constituents. Librarians are often slow or reluctant to eliminate collections that even a few patrons are still using. But as every library has limitations, asking these questions can help you focus your collection budget and provide justifications for making changes. While your library won't know the actual use of its eBook collection until it's purchased and available for use, it's likely that the return on investment for this collection will be higher than that for several other lower-use collections your library is currently purchasing. Once again, you will want to prepare messaging for your stakeholders if you are making a change in purchasing.

SELECTING TITLES

Once you've identified funding sources and established a basic budget allocation framework, you'll need to start working on how you will select the materials you want to have ready for your opening day collection. You may have already developed a preliminary plan for this, since you would have needed to know the average cost per title and similar information to determine how much funding to allocate, or to estimate the size of your preliminary collection. But with the funding secured, you're able to really dig into what's available for you to select from your vendors.

The good news is that library eBook vendors are all spending significant time and resources on collection development. They are working with a range of large and small publishers to determine what they want to, and are able to, provide to libraries, based on what librarians are asking for and what publishers are making available. You have multiple options available in terms of selection methodology. For example, you can use prepared lists from the vendor. You can use vendor lists and supplement selection based on your own added criteria. You can turn over all the selection duties to a vendor based on parameters you supply. You can select all the titles individually through searches of the vendor database, or employ a variety of these methods at the same time.

In terms of supplied lists, vendors are producing lists of titles for librarians to select from based on what is happening in the consumer marketplace and what librarians are purchasing and what lists library staff are suggesting the vendor to compile. There are lists based on national best-seller lists, what is selling most frequently for each vendor, what titles have been reviewed in standard review journals, titles in series, what titles are proving most popular in other library systems, and a wide range of other subject and audience-based lists. Depending on the type of collection you wish to start with, using these lists can be an easy way to get started with an opening collection.

For example, if your library wanted to launch its first eBook collection by focusing on adult fiction and best-selling titles, you could easily use vendor lists to purchase an opening collection. Vendors will likely have lists of titles on national best-seller lists, as well as lists of popular backlist titles, lists featuring top-selling authors, top series titles, and similar lists. Because library vendors work with a large number of libraries, vendors are also tracking what libraries purchase and are producing lists of titles based on what titles they are selling to libraries. Any or all of these lists can be used to create a beginning collection of eBooks.

You can also use a combination of vendor-supplied lists along with library staff selection. If you wish to use a combination approach, lists plus library selection, using your own collection data on what circulates well in physical format is a great starting point. For example, do you know your top-circulating authors within the scope of your opening collection? If so, you can compare your top-circulating authors with the lists of top-selling authors from the vendor. Any authors you don't find on the vendor lists, you can run separate searches for in the vendor database. The authors you don't find will likely be ones who have a more regional focus and won't show up on the national lists. Likewise, for whatever collection you are starting with, do you know your top-circulating titles in physical format? Again, you can look for titles not covered in the vendor-supplied lists. In general, if you are using vendor lists and want or need to augment what you find on those lists, looking through the vendor database for local authors or local presses is an excellent way to expand your search and find titles you wish to offer to your patrons. Any time you are looking to expand your title pool for a collection, look for other methods that will find titles that resonate with your local community and fit into your collection scope.

If you or your staff don't have the time to make the individual selections, you can often let the vendor manage the selection process. As with similar vendor-led selection processes already in place for print collections, your library provides the vendor with the amount that can be spent in each area, as well as any other parameters or restrictions regarding the composition of the collection, and the vendor can then supply you with lists to review and approve for purchase. Depending on the collection parameters you provide to vendors, they will likely use the lists already described here as the foundation of the collection they will build for you.

One of the most important things you can do when building a collection is to ask for what you need from the vendor. Vendors want to help you purchase materials, and they will provide whatever assistance they can to you. Like the lists they are already curating within their acquisition system, they may have other tools or expertise that can support you as you start building your collection. They may be able to build special lists for you or offer other assistance. They may also take suggestions from you and your staff about what changes to their process would make the selection process easier for you in the future.

If you are making all selection decisions locally, library vendors will usually provide access to their entire list of available titles for you to use to select titles for your library. Generally, as stated in Chapter 3, the vendors provide a shopping cart service from their web portal, similar to what you may already use for your print collections. Vendors will have tools to tell you which titles are on multiple lists, which titles you have already purchased, which titles you have in a different cart, and so on. Vendors are developing sophisticated search engines in order to get you to the eBooks you want, trying to make it as easy as possible for you to use the tools they provide to help connect you to potential purchases. While you are, of course, limited to purchasing the titles provided by the vendor(s) you work with, the increasing ease of using these tools can help streamline the selection process for your staff.

One issue to note here, and mentioned elsewhere in the book as well, is that the subject and other descriptors for the eBooks are not coming from a standardized place. In general, library staff like standardization. They like putting similar materials next to each other on physical shelves, and they like describing material in the same way with the same words by using standardized subject headings such as Library of Congress subject headings. This helps patrons get to exactly what they want, and librarians have years of practical experience that supports the value of structures, naming practices, consistent metadata, and access points in making books and other materials easy to find by a wide range of users.

However, when you are purchasing your books from most eBook vendors, as well as directly from publishers, the descriptors for eBooks are not coming from entities like the Library of Congress, or from a shared list of standard terms and descriptors. Instead, the terms used to describe and provide access to eBooks are most likely to be coming directly from the publishers. What publishers want from their descriptors is to entice customers to purchase their titles. They are not necessarily looking to provide comprehensive access to multiple subject headings, or to provide complete descriptive access to each title. As trends pop up, publishers change their marketing, and so do their descriptors to take advantage of the terms and brands that are currently popular. Sometimes these descriptors are helpful in searching a vendor's database, but sometimes they may add a layer of complexity, since there may be a wide range of overlapping terms to choose from. Similar titles from different publishers will not necessarily be described the same way, and older titles and newer titles may also not use the same descriptors as trends can change over time. However, if you are not getting the search results you expect when searching the vendor site, check in with your vendor. Their collection management staff can help you navigate and hopefully pin-point search strategies within their database that get you to the results you want. You will also be giving them feedback on how you want, and expect, the system to work, which will hopefully lead to changes in this area.

ORDERING

Once you have a cart or multiple carts of titles that you want to purchase, you are ready to order the materials for your library. As part of this step, there are at least a few more issues to sort through to make the ordering process go smoothly. Since the carts of titles you have selected are part of the vendor's tool, there should be an easy process in place to confirm to the vendor that these are the titles that you wish to purchase. That purchase confirmation will then naturally trigger the billing and invoicing process. To make sure this process goes smoothly, you will want to work with the vendor to ensure that the necessary financial processes are in place to connect the purchase information from the vendor with the library's financial system and integrated library system (ILS). In particular, your library may want or need exact title, quantity, and cost per item information loaded into your ILS acquisition or other financial system, or you may just need a cost rollup amount entered into your system, the number of titles ordered on a particular date, and total cost for the entire order. These are steps that you will want to set up in advance with the vendor, but you will also need to monitor the process as you start ordering materials to make sure everything is working as intended. As your ordering process gets under way, you should be able to get useful data from this system, but only if it's working as expected.

If purchasing these types of materials, that is, individual digital objects, is new to you or your library system, take the time to pilot the ordering method from start to finish so you don't need to backtrack later to add additional information. Most librarians have lots of experience now with contracting with database vendors. And of course you have lots of experience with purchasing physical materials. However, purchasing an eBook collection with a vendor is part online database and part physical in its execution. Ordering individual eBook titles on an ongoing basis is similar to the ordering of physical materials, but because there's no arrival of the item in a box, there may be additional steps that need to be worked out. You aren't able to open the box and confirm that everything that was ordered was delivered and is in working condition. The process for verifying eBook orders and otherwise managing this part of the process is obviously different from ordering physical materials. If you have other staff whose focus is on the financial end of the library's business and you are purchasing in this manner for the first time, you may want to consult with that financial staff to make sure they see no issues with how you are reporting the purchases of eBooks. It's better to have everyone on the same page as you move into this new area rather than to find out that there are issues with your purchasing process: issues that might delay payment to the vendors or limit your ability to get new eBooks to your patrons once the first books in the collection have been made available to them.

If you are contracting with the vendor to provide MARC records through an affiliated vendor, any eBook order will trigger a MARC record order from that affiliated vendor. Your process for retrieving the MARC records once they are available should be planned in advance. You can access the MARC records from an FTP site, or your library may already have a subscription to vendors for other valued-added services like cataloging services, and could fold your eBook MARC records into that process. Depending on what you're already doing in this area, there is likely to be nothing out of ordinary with the billing or invoicing for MARC records, but it will be good to check on at least for the first month or two. These MARC records are how your patrons will be able to find your eBooks in your catalog, and you'll want to make sure this process is working so your patrons will have the access to the collection that they expect to find.

In most cases, vendors try to make the ordering process as simple as possible. They know that this needs to work smoothly to ensure that you will continue to purchase materials from them, and that they get paid in a timely manner for materials they've sold to your library. Most of your staff time related to billing and invoicing is spent making sure that you create a workflow that meets your system's requirements for financial reporting, and that you monitor it periodically to make sure it continues to work smoothly. You may already have a similar practice in place, and may simply need to expand that to include your new eBook vendors and related processes.

PROVIDING ACCESS

In Chapter 3, the basic components that are needed to be able to provide access to your eBook collection were discussed. In order for your patrons to actually find and circulate the titles you've purchased, you'll need online tools to make that happen. Whether you're building your own platform or using a vendor product, you'll want to make sure you dedicate time and staff expertise to this part of your project.

If you are working with vendors, some, but not all, of the main access and delivery points may be part of the package you purchase from them. Most of the current vendors provide a public-facing web interface that can serve as the primary portal to your eBook collection if you choose to use it. These vendor sites include patron account management, access to titles and lists, and search functionality. They are increasingly reader-friendly and can be easily customized by library staff. Many offer users the ability to rate and review titles, enhancing the overall experience of using their sites.

In addition to traditional websites, vendors offer separate apps that are available in the major app stores. Patrons with mobile devices may find these to be the preferred method of accessing eBooks since apps are designed for mobile users and allow patrons to get eBooks when they are on the go. These apps are often an important way for patrons using mobile devices to access your library's eBook collection, and are another important part of proving access to your eBook collection across the wide range of devices your patrons are using.

Many libraries use the vendor-provided website and apps as their primary access points for patrons, and see no need to create any additional points for access to their collections. For instance, some libraries decide not to make their eBook collection accessible through their library catalog. Instead, the vendor sites are accessed just like any other databases or online resources on the library's website. Patrons provide their barcode to authenticate, confirming that they are eligible to use the collection, and then can use the vendor site just as they would the library's own site to look for materials and to check them out. If this is the level of access that meets the needs of your patrons, then this is a good approach for you to use. You may have a small collection, a small user base, or limited technical or collection staff time to dedicate to additional online access. If you start with this basic online access plan, you'll want to be prepared to evaluate and potentially adjust it as your collection develops. This model does become more complicated if you have more than one vendor or platform, because your patrons will need to check each of the vendor sites separately to determine what's available. If you're working with multiple vendors, or start with one and add another one as your collection expands, you'll want to evaluate the plan to have your patrons only use vendor websites for access to make sure you understand how it works from their perspective. It may still be the best way to offer access to your collections, or you may want to consider adding the MARC records to your catalog or looking at other options as your service matures.

As noted in chapter 2, library vendors can provide MARC records for a fee for the eBooks you purchase. Taking advantage of these MARC records will allow you to provide access to your eBooks in your library catalog, which is usually the primary place that your patrons expect to find all of your collection. When they search for a title or subject in your catalog, all of the copies you own, across all formats, would be in one place, and your patrons would be able to select what they prefer once they've seen all the options. Having your eBooks in your catalog supports patrons who are format-agnostic; they didn't necessarily come looking for an eBook, but just want a copy of the book and will take what's available. Without your eBooks in the catalog, those patrons will not be able to take advantage of this new format, since they may not want to take the additional steps needed to go to the separate vendor websites.

If you do decide to include the MARC records in your catalog, you'll want to take a step back and consider what type of experience you'll be providing your patrons as they find eBooks in their search results. The MARC records will make the books discoverable the same way that your physical materials are, so that part should be pretty straightforward. eBooks then should have the same display in your catalog search results as your other materials so patrons will be able to determine which format they're most interested in. But once your patrons find all the copies of the book you own, you'll need to make sure that they can be distinguished from your print and audiobook copies of the same title. You probably already have format icons or text descriptions to do this for your other formats, so you'll just need to expand that for your eBook collection.

Once your patrons have found an eBook they want in your catalog, you'll need to consider how they'll be able to access the book. For your physical collection, patrons can either place a reserve on the item to have it held for them, have it sent to their library from another location, or they can find the call number and go to the shelves to pick up the book themselves. eBooks are similar in that your patrons will expect to be able to check out the book and get it onto their devices if it's available, or place a reserve on it if it's not available and your policies allow that.

One challenge here is that, unless you have integrated the vendor's API into your catalog, your catalog won't be able to display the availability information for the title, or allow the patron to download the title directly from the bibliographic record. In most cases, this is where libraries connect back to the vendor website. Patrons find the eBook in your catalog, and then instead of requesting or reserving the item there, they are directed back to item record in the vendor website, where they can see if the title is available and either reserve it or request it and move it to their device.

If this is the model you use to provide access in the catalog, you'll want to make sure you walk through all the steps from the patron's perspective. Since patrons will need to move from your catalog to the vendor website to complete the process, at some point they'll need to provide their library card for authentication. In many cases, when you move from the library website to a vendor database, you enter your library card or other information before you can access anything in the database. For your eBooks, that would mean that a patron who only wants to know if the book is available will have to enter his or her card number to see anything about the book. On the other hand, for your physical collections, patrons can browse your catalog and see availability and other information, and probably only need to give you their card information to place a reserve or check out the copy if it's available. This is one of the paradoxes of the online eBook collection; if you treat it like a vendor database (which is it) you're probably not providing the same type of access to eBooks as you do to your physical collection. On the other hand, since the books are online, not on your shelves, you may have to authenticate at a different place in the process, possibly based on your practice for your online resources or your vendor requirements for accessing their databases. There's no perfect answer to how to manage this part of the process. You'll just want to do what you can to minimize unnecessary restrictions or barriers for your patrons, and still provide a smooth and consistent process for moving from your catalog for discovery to the vendor website for access. You will also want to be sure that your patrons can move back to the library's website easily from the vendor website.

Another thing to note here is that, since your patrons check out their eBooks from the vendor website, their account information is managed there also. They'll need to check what books they have out, what's on hold, and their due dates on the vendor site instead of tracking that on your site with the rest of their materials. If you're working with multiple vendors, they'll probably have to manage accounts with each of them separately, and still manage them on the vendor websites and outside of their regular library account.

As with other parts of this process, all of this can become more complicated as you work with multiple vendors. Each may provide a slightly different experience here as it comes to authentication, ability to link to item level displays, and amount of availability information. No matter how you work through these issues, remember to step back and walk through it from the patron's perspective. Do your catalog text, icons, and other links clearly tell them what's happening, which vendor collection they're using, and what action they're taking if they click on a button or link? Does your patron account page in your catalog remind them that their eBooks aren't included there? It's easy to forget that this is a new experience for many of our users, and that this can be a complex process with lots of new steps. What used to be all in one place may now be managed across several vendor websites, and that increases if you also provide downloadable or streaming music, video, or audiobooks. This is definitely one of the more challenging aspects of our current eBook environment, whether you're working with vendor tools or developing your own platforms.

As you can see, all of this can make for a bumpy patron experience, since your users may need to coordinate across several sites to fully know what's happening with the books they're reading. While some patrons may adjust to this process, it's likely that you'll get patron feedback about the complexity of the overall experience of using your library's eBook collection. While there may not be much you can do about this, consider spending some time walking through this process step by step so you and your staff can understand the experience from the user perspective. That should provide an opportunity to look for ways to streamline the process, and may also provide some insights on where to focus staff training or what to cover in public programming.

As mentioned several times already, one of the bright spots in this otherwise-complicated landscape is the increasing availability of vendor APIs. A number of eBook vendors are beginning to provide APIs which facilitate data sharing between the vendor site and your library website or catalog. Instead of needing to direct a patron to the vendor website to find out about the availability of a title, review account information, or check out a book, an API allows you to bring that data to your site and integrate it into the other parts of your display. When a patron looks for a book, using an API will let you display the data about the number of copies, the waiting list, and similar information the same way you present it for your physical collection. Using an API will let you display the eBooks a patron has checked out and their due dates alongside the same information about their print items, so they only need to check one place to see what's happening with their library materials. Because they have authenticated with their library card to see their account information in your catalog, they don't need to do it again to see their eBooks. And since they don't need to authenticate to see availability in your catalog, they won't need to do it to see it for eBooks either.

Implementing an API will probably require you, someone on your staff, or another person you have access to have web development expertise, and will depend on whether APIs are available from your eBook vendors and what's possible with your ILS and web-site. What you're able to integrate will depend on what data points are included in the API, and how they line up with the data that you provide your patrons about your physical collections. The integration may lead you to reexamine the way you provide this information in your catalog and on your website, so you should be prepared to make some changes, or at least review your options, should you decide to implement vendor APIs. They can be a great way to integrate your eBooks into your broader collection and service strategy, as well as move your patrons away from relying on the vendor website experience and back to your library site. But they do add new integration points to your library catalog that will need to be maintained and updated, since you're not just linking over to the vendor website to manage all of the patron activity. Like any part of this process, the API can help streamline the steps for the patron and improve the overall patron experience, but can bring new challenges as well.

CIRCULATION RULES

As you start planning to launch your collection, you'll need to spend some time thinking about circulation rules and how you'll manage this part of your service. Having at least a basic understanding of how you expect to make materials available to your patrons, and how you plan to address pressures on your collection from high use, will help you set your overall circulation strategy.

You already have a framework in place for circulating your physical collection, so you have a place to start your work. Do you want your eBook collection to operate exactly the same as your physical collection, using the same circulation rules? Or do you want or need the rules to be different for eBooks because this collection feels different for staff and patrons? Do you already have other online collections (audiobooks, music, etc.) that you need to align with, or will this be your first collection that needs this new approach?

The first questions you'll want to ask are about who will have access to your eBook collection. Who will you allow to check out books from this collection? The technology exists to allow anyone who has a library card number in your system to be able to use your collection. Is that okay? Do your neighboring systems allow your patrons to do the same? Are there any political or community-based reasons that would require you to limit eBook lending to the patrons who live in your funding district? Your options here may be limited by your vendor contract, as well as by your local library structures and resource-sharing agreements. You may want the same patrons who can use your physical collection to have access to your eBook collection, or you may need to approach these two collections differently. This can be a complicated issue for libraries, and it's one you'll want to have addressed, and cleared with your stakeholders, before you launch your collection.

The next questions you'll want to consider are about how many copies you'll make available to your patrons. How many eBooks will you allow your patrons to check out at one time? Will you allow them to establish waiting lists, and how long will those lists be able to be? This decision may depend on how big your opening collection is, as well as on the practices you already have in place for your physical collection. If you are starting your collection with a modest number of eBooks, you may want to start with a modest limit for your patrons. If you are certain that you are launching your eBook collection permanently, or have a larger budget to spend to launch your collection, the question of how many eBooks and copies you'll have available may influence the number of eBooks you let your patrons check out at a time. Even though you are just beginning your eBook service, what circumstances would induce you to change and hopefully increase your checkout limits as your collection changes and grows is an excellent thing to plan for. It's not essential, but putting the thinking and planning in at launch will make it easier for you to implement these types of changes as you reach those stages. This is another area where you may want to consider how the number of eBooks you make available per patron aligns with your practice for print copies. With possibly lower limits for eBooks, your patrons who become eBook-only readers will have less access to your collection than your print readers, and may raise questions about equitable access that you should be prepared to speak to if asked.

You'll also want to consider how long you'll let your patrons keep the books. What will be your loan period for eBooks? As you can see with many of the issues around picking a vendor and setting up your service, you have multiple options based on what works best for your system. For loan periods, you probably do want to mirror the loan periods you have for physical material if your vendor supports that option. Some vendors also have a limited number of loan period options. You can choose usually 7, 14, or 21 days. If you need to impose a limit on who can check out items from your collection (e.g., excluding patrons who live outside your funding district because of political or contractual reasons), or how many eBooks your patrons can check-out because your opening collection isn't very big and you want as many of your patrons as possible have access to eBooks, your reasons are pretty easy to explain. Your patrons may not like the reasons but they are logical, and based either on external factors like library jurisdictions or contracts, or on short-term situations that will hopefully change in the future. However, a different loan period for eBooks from what you use for your physical material can be harder to explain. With eBooks, the content is the same, only the delivery method is different. For example, titles like *Mockingjay, To Kill a Mockingbird*, and *Fifty Shades of Grey* should all circulate three weeks in eBook form if they circulate for three weeks in physical form. Or two weeks, or four weeks—whatever the standard length time is for your physical materials. The book is the same regardless of the package, and the books don't get shorter or easier to read just because they're in a digital format, so the amount of time you allow your patrons to read in one format should be the same in the other format.

WHAT HAPPENS WHEN THERE ARE PROBLEMS?

Sometimes, things just don't work. What will you do when things go awry? For instance, what happens when an eBook file is corrupted and the patron can't open the file to read the book? What happens when a patron can't get one of your eBooks to his or her device because he or she has downloaded the wrong format? What are your expectations as to who will deal with the issues? Who will work with the patrons to address these questions: you, your front-line staff, your IT or technical staff, your vendor, or some combination of those groups? While these issues may not happen very often, they're an important part of your overall customer service strategy and should be considered as you start or expand your service. You can ask your vendor for their most common eBook issues and how they are typically resolved and which party is responsible for the resolution. Some of this information will come from your contract. In your contract, the vendor may outline, for example, what to do if an eBook file is reportedly corrupted. Knowing what the vendor sees as common issues can be used to train staff and to create an eBook issue workflow on the library's end.

Since you're working with a vendor, you'll want to take the time to check that their timetable for addressing patron questions is what you want, expect, and need, especially related to questions only they can solve, like corrupted files. Some vendors have given some control back to libraries to address some of the basic problems that can happen as part of the eBook lending process. For instance, it's possible that when a patron checks out an eBook, the file can be corrupted. The vendor should be able to fix the file or get a new file from the publisher, but now the patron who had it checked out has lost his or her place in the queue. Depending on the vendor you may have the ability to shuffle the queue so that your patron with the corrupted file can have the next available copy of the eBook. This may be the same service that you would provide for a patron using your print materials who receives a damaged copy of a book he or she wishes to check out, but it will function differently for your eBook collection.

You already have models in place for the types of questions that arise with your physical collections. You may have staff assigned to collect fines and overdue fees for materials that are returned late, or not at all. You know how to handle books that come back with minor damage, or that need to be withdrawn because they are in such poor condition that they can no longer be used by other patrons. eBooks don't need most of those types of support or staff intervention, but they bring their own set of customer service questions that will need to be addressed. It's possible that the same staff members who handle the questions for your physical collections can handle these eBook challenges also, or you may need to work on a new approach to some of these questions. You'll want to consider the staff who will be best positioned to field the patron questions, and either make the needed changes or refer the issue to the vendor for questions that need their attention. When the issue is fixed, you or your staff need to follow up with the patron. While it can be a fairly straightforward process, it's not the same as fine payment or damaged print materials, and may take some adjustment to your staffing and training to ensure that you have this part covered. Understanding what options are available from the vendor and what you have the capacity to support will help you determine how you want to implement this part of your service strategy.

CONCLUSION

If you contract with an established vendor, it will have dedicated project managers with experience in setting up eBook systems in a variety of types of libraries that will work with you through the launch of your collection. The vendors will have checklists of issues that need to be decided as part of the setup process, and areas that need to be considered as your library moves through the steps that will make your collection available to your users. Some of the decisions may be simple and straightforward and can build on work you've already started as part of your planning process, including your budgeting allocation decisions. However, some questions that you'll need to consider may need additional time for your staff to think through, as there are potential connections with other parts of your collection that may need some additional consideration. While not exhaustive, a checklist of decisions or questions that need to be made as part of launching your eBook collection is included at the end of this chapter (see Figure 4.1.) The checklist is designed to help you track the decisions that need to be made regardless of the vendor or vendors you choose. The list can also be used as a way to assign staff to parts of the process as well as a way to inform your stakeholders of the decisions you are making.

Funding
    Percentage of budget allocated for first-time purchases of titles
    Percentage of budget allocated for repurchasing of titles that have expired because they have reached the allocated circulation limits or time periods
    Percentage of budget allocated to respond to patron requests and to purchase additional "copies" of eBooks of those titles that patrons are really interested in

Patron limits
    Definition of who can use the library's eBook collection.
        Geographic restrictions
        Fine or fee status
        Other restricted users
    Length of loan period(s)
    How many eBooks can be checked out by one patron at one time?
    How many holds can a patron place at one time?
    How many titles can a patron have on a "wishlist" for future use?

Ordering process
    Methods to transfer ordering information from vendor into library's financial system

Access
    Vendor website and app setup
        Library logo/branding
        Front page decisions
            Content on the front page
            Curated lists or bookshelves
    Bibliographic information in the library catalog
        Methods to import MARC records into the library catalog
        Icon to denote eBook
        API integration

Customer service
    Types of patron issues or problems to be fixed at library
        Staff training needed to support this decision
    Types of patron issues or problems to be fixed by the vendor
        Service agreements needed to support this decision

Figure 4.1   Checklist of Decisions to Be Made When Implementing an eBook Collection

CHAPTER 5

Connecting Patrons to Your eBook Collection

Purchasing eBooks and creating a collection isn't all you need to do in order to make an impact with your users. While developing a plan for launching your collection is an important first step, you'll want to make sure you have a longer-term, sustainable approach to promoting your collection and services for eBook readers as well. In order to really reach your patrons, including new patrons who might not be currently using the library, you will want to develop a promotion or marketing strategy. You will also want to work to connect your eBooks to the other services you already offer for readers of all ages.

PROMOTION AND MARKETING

Integrating your eBook collection into your ongoing promotion of library services will be important to its overall success. One of the most important things you'll need to determine is what you will be promoting. Will you be focusing on target audiences? Will you create specialized messages, seeking to reach those target audiences you identified in your initial plan? Will you focus generally on connecting people to this new format, making sure that your patrons know that you now offer eBooks? Will you be focusing on your expanded service for readers, adding this new format to all of the ways you already market your collection to them? Will you be promoting this new way to get books for homework assignments, for recreational reading, or for travel? All of these are potential ways to promote your new collection, and they all potentially connect with a different group of patrons. Taking some time to consider your most important message(s) will help you develop a basic promotion strategy that should take you from the launch of your service to a longer-term way to connect with current and new users.

Earlier in this book it was recommended that you start your planning process by connecting with your patrons to get a better understanding of what they're interested in. As you develop your promotion and marketing plan, refer back to the initial feedback you received from patrons. You can use the feedback from the start of your project to help you determine which messages will be most meaningful to your users. You solicited patron input on what types of materials they thought they'd be using. You may also have actual patron use data if you're developing your promotional plan after your service is already under way. While you'll want a general message for all of your patrons and potential new users letting them know that you now have eBooks to get this started, you'll want to work on more targeted messages to reach specific groups of patrons you know will be interested in this service. If your patrons have told you that they'll be reading primarily fiction, then beginning with a promotional plan that reaches out to fiction readers will be a good way to start getting the word out. If your patrons have told you that they're already purchasing eBooks from commercial vendors, then letting those patrons know that you now have this format available also will be a key message to reach that audience. You can build on your promotional plan as you expand your collection, especially as you start adding more titles or new content areas. And as your patrons start using the collection and you can see their use patterns and interests, you'll be able to adjust your messaging to meet their needs.

As you develop your promotion and marketing plan, you'll want to make sure you're using all of the appropriate channels to reach your patrons. You may already have a number of methods already in place to connect with your community: your website, posters or handouts in your library or posted at community locations, social media, a library newsletter, a column in the local paper, or other methods. You and your staff may have regular visits at the local schools or senior centers, or you may work with community organizations. All of those strategies are part of the way you connect with your users and promote library services, and you should evaluate all of them as potential places to share the news about your eBook collection. Each of these options is unique; some allow you to plan and schedule regular, ongoing messages to reach your current patrons, and others have your staff connecting with current and potential new users with a personal connection, often at a community location. But with all of these options you have the opportunity to focus on the audience you're trying to reach and tailor a message for that group.

If you're looking to reach the general reader who may already be a library patron, your regular promotional channels are a good place to start. These channels already focus on a broad range of library services, and your eBook collection will just be a new one to add to the mix. You can share information about the new format, the types of materials that will be added, or the programs you've planned to help people with questions about accessing library eBooks with their devices. This will let you highlight the format as well as the broad collection areas you're starting with without needing to go into too much detail in any specific area. Posters in your library, a message on your website and social media, a column in your local paper all reach this broad audience. These are great ways to start spreading the news about your library's new or expanded eBook collection.

If you're looking to connect with specific audiences, you'll have opportunities to tailor your message within your current promotional opportunities also. If you're working with book clubs, school groups, community centers, or planning author programs, you can easily bring promotional materials to those events, making sure these audiences know that you've added a new collection that may be of interest to them. This gives you an opportunity to connect directly with patrons most likely to be interested in what your library has added, and is a great way to listen to what messages are working and which aren't connecting as well. Perhaps you're visiting a senior center and the people you talk with at the center express an interest in eBooks. But they indicate that they're not familiar with using devices to get access to eBooks. This gives you a good chance to review your promotional materials to make sure they include information about any programs you're offering about how to get library eBooks onto eReaders and other devices or at least message about library staff assistance always being available. If you're visiting a school and learn that all of the students now have school-issued devices, that's a reminder to make sure your promotion to this audience mentions that your eBooks are available for the devices they're using. The ability to adjust and align your message for these specific, high-impact audiences will be an important part of making a longer-term change in the way users understand what's now available from the library and how it aligns with their interests and needs.

One thing to remember, of course, is that the promotion you're doing needs to reflect the collection and service you're planning to offer and can support. If you're not planning to add much to your collection to support students and homework, then your promotional materials shouldn't promise that you can meet all of their homework needs. If you are not currently purchasing much for young children, then you'll want to be clear about what you're promoting if you talk about eBooks during your storytime programs. You can let storytime patrons know that your library will have great books for the adults, but limited materials for young readers at this point. It's easy to want to promote a broad "we have eBooks!" message and in some places, that's just the message you need. But if you're talking with an audience that mostly has Kindles, Nooks, or other proprietary devices and you aren't actually purchasing any of the propriety file types they can use, then you're just leading them to a dissatisfactory experience with the library. It will then be more difficult to get those potential patrons back when you add more file types or even if they change devices. One unsuccessful transaction or experience is often hard to overcome. To make your promotional plan successful, you'll want to make sure you're aligning with what your audience needs to know, and not promising things you're not able to provide, especially as you get started.

REACHING CURRENT LIBRARY PATRONS

Many of the standard ways that libraries promote their collection and services primarily reach patrons who already use the library in some way. That's a good thing, in that it's a way to make sure that your primary users, the people who are already using your services, are aware of all of their options. They're the ones most likely to use them, and are also likely to share the information with others in the community. They help your library spread the word about what you do. Having a consistent strategy in place to reach them, at launch and beyond, will help you grow your service, and make connections between your physical and online collections.

Since your current patrons are probably at least semi-regular visitors to your library buildings and website, making sure you have consistent messaging in those venues will be an important way to connect with them. They may not regularly ask staff for assistance, and may think they know what the library has to offer and so may not be actively looking for new services. Having a consistent, long-term strategy in place to reach these important patrons will be worth the effort, since they're already connected to the library and interested in finding books to read or to support their research or personal needs. Providing additional ways to get books will be a welcome message for many of these regular users of your library.

REACHING POTENTIAL NEW USERS

Adding an eBook collection also provides a unique opportunity to reach out and bring new users to the library. These could be users who don't come to the library because it's not geographically close to them, or who have other challenges with getting to the library building during the hours it's open. They could be patrons who like the fine-free access to the collection that eBooks can provide. Or they may be people who like the ability to get a new book at any time instead of needing to schedule a trip to the library. They may be eBook readers already and would be happy to have another place to get eBooks. There may be some people who have not been reading regularly, but are returning to reading now that this new, convenient way is available to them. Whatever the reason they're not currently using your library service or physical collections, you're providing them with a new way to think about the library, and hopefully to use your library again. As you look at ways to promote your collection to them, you'll want to consider what messages will be most effective and listen for the things that are most meaningful to them. If convenience is important to them, that's an important message for your library to focus on, highlighting the 24/7 access to books, and the ability to check out and return books without needing to make a trip to the library. If cost is a factor, the fine-free access and ability to get books for free will be important to promote. Of course, these messages may be important for your current patrons as well, so it's possible for your promotion for new users to resonate with all of your library patrons.

As you reach out to new users, you'll want to consider the process to access eBooks from their perspective. Assuming they're not current library patrons, will they need to get a library card to access the collection, and how does that process work if they can't (or don't want to) come to the library to sign up for a card? How can they get assistance if they're not able to come to a library program, or come to the library to talk with a staff member? As you're working on connecting with these new or returning library users, consider what this looks like for them, and make sure your promotional messages are ones that will resonate with them, and that actually reflect the experience they'll have if they try to use your service. If they need to visit a library building to sign up for a card before they can use this online service, make sure that is clear in your messaging. If you have staff available online to provide assistance, or a phone line they can call, include that in your promotion so your remote patrons will know that your staff's expertise will be available to them even if they never come to a library building.

TIMING OF PROMOTIONAL CAMPAIGNS

Another thing to consider is the timing of your promotional strategy. Your first impulse may be to do a big marketing campaign as soon as your collection is available, since you want your whole community to know about this new service. In many cases, that may be the right move for your library and your patrons. It's an exciting change, and a great way to get more books into the hands of more readers. But just as you do with other collections or services you offer, you may also want to consider a "soft launch." Making the collection available with only limited promotion to begin with has advantages. For example, during the brief period of the soft launch, you and your staff can have a chance to get familiar with how they'll need to support and manage the service before you bring in a larger audience. This would let you work with a few patrons on their customer service and device questions. Staff can get a feel for how patrons are discovering your collection before making a larger push and moving toward an increase in users. One challenge when launching a new collection or service is to make sure you're able to actually support the demand for what you're adding. If you and your staff aren't ready to assist patrons, or you're starting with a small collection and are concerned that everything would get checked out right away, all of the new patrons you bring in with your big promotional campaign may be disappointed in what you're actually able to offer, at least at first.

Timing your promotion when you're ready to support your new users is key, and making sure your marketing messages are aligned with the appropriate channels and patron groups will help you make sure your messages are meeting your need. Launching a new eBook collection is a great opportunity to strengthen your connection with your current users, as well as a way to reach new or former users. To make the most of your promotion, having a thoughtful plan in place that highlights what you're able to deliver and support for each audience will help you make the most of this exciting opportunity.

STANDALONE KIOSKS

One of the challenges of connecting your patrons with your eBook collection is that they can't see the books when they come to the library and browse the shelves. An additional issue is that your patrons will need to have some way to get eBooks from the vendor website or your library's local platform to their devices. As a way to address these issues, some vendors provide standalone kiosks that patrons can use to view and access eBooks. The types of kiosks and standalone access points vary by vendor, but in general, the goal of these products is to make your "invisible" eBooks visible to your patrons. The kiosks allow patrons to browse your eBook collection and often allow them to check out the books also. These types of free-standing displays can help you promote your collection, allowing patrons to browse what's available for check-out while in your library or at a community location.

As a way to make your collection more visible to patrons and to help address access issues, these vendor kiosks can be useful. However, there are also challenges with using them in your library. If you are contracting with multiple vendors, each will probably offer you their own kiosk, so you may find you'll need multiple, different kiosks to provide equitable access to all the parts of your collection. If your eBook collection has felt invisible to patrons, a kiosk that highlights only part of your eBook collection still may be a worthwhile investment, but you'll need to be ready to assist patrons with any questions or concerns they have about accessing all of your eBooks, not just those with the separate kiosk. And, of course, these kiosks take up physical space in your library, which may be at a premium. You want to have this in a prominent place, or near other parts of the collection that your eBook readers may use, but in many libraries that space can be difficult to find. You'll also need to understand what roles and responsibilities your library takes on with this equipment, and what remains with the vendor.

It's also possible for you to create your own eBook station or kiosk. It would be as easy as dedicating a computer in a prominent location to this service. The landing page for this computer could be the vendor website or the eBook page on your own website, and it could have any software that's needed to transfer eBooks to a user device already installed and ready to use. This model lets you highlight multiple vendors and more closely connects to the experience your patrons would have when they're using eBooks on their own devices, but it does require using library computers and other equipment to provide the service.

You may find that your patrons prefer to search for and check out their eBooks from home or other non-library locations and aren't as interested in accessing them in the library building, and that's part of the learning process with your new collection. Alternatively, you may have community members who need to use a library computer to access eBooks because they don't have one at home, and these in-library models can help support their ability to use your collection. The vendor-provided kiosks and library-supported workstation both provide in-library opportunities to promote the collection and provide access, and may be welcome parts of your overall strategy, or they may end up being more complicated to manage than you want to support and with only limited impact. They're worth exploring as options as ways to address the promotion and access questions, even if they don't turn out to be a fit for your service.

STAFF TRAINING AND SUPPORT

When adding an eBook collection, it's important to remember what is known about so many other parts of library work: library staff is the key connector between patrons and your collections and services. As you start your planning for the launch of your eBook collection, you'll want to make sure you and your staff are prepared to assist patrons as they start to use your new collection. You want to have a plan in place to help everyone on the library staff build and maintain the skills they'll need to work with your patrons both at the start and as the collection and service matures.

With so many other things to consider as you get under way, it's easy to leave this part of the process until the very end, or underestimate what might be needed to get your staff up to speed and comfortable with all of the new things they may need to know. While many of your staff may be excited to work with patrons in this new way, it's possible that you'll have staff who are reluctant to take this on. You may have staff whose technical skills may not be strong enough to jump right in to the new tools without some additional support. And just as you have patrons who may question why you are adding eBooks, you may have staff who question this also, and may not see or welcome their role in supporting this new service. As with any change of this nature, having staff involved early in the process, setting clear service expectations, and being prepared to help staff gain new skills so they can help your patrons will be the key to your success.

One way to get everyone on the same page is to develop a vision statement or similar statement of service that covers the scope of what you're planning to offer, and clarifying how staff can support that goal. You may already have service statements in place at your library and could add information about supporting eBooks to what you already use, or you could develop something just to clarify what your staff expectations are related to your new collection. A sample version of a service statement is added at the end of this chapter (see Figure 5.1) to give you an idea of what this could look like.

Supporting eBook users can bring some new challenges to customer service. It may require staff to use new tools to help patrons find something to read. They may need to ask new questions, not just "do you want a paperback or hard-cover copy?" but now "what device will you be reading this on?" They may need to get involved with file download and device setup questions, which could be completely new to them. One of the more difficult areas in this new environment is when a staff with lower technical skills needs to work with patrons who are also less comfortable with the technology needed to use eBooks. There can be as many things that staff needs to know to check on and to make sure the process is working as well as there can be for the patron. A patron's computer and/or other devices, vendor files and websites, e-mail notifications, and digital rights management (DRM) can all be challenges that library staff needs to navigate in order to help the patron. When both library staff and the patron have limited skills and confidence in this area, even straight-forward situations can become more complicated. Investing in staff training and support, and establishing clear expectations for service, can help your staff improve their skills and be more confident when working with patrons, especially with those who need some additional support.

A good customer service approach can address all of these new questions, but it may take a while for staff to get used to these new questions and to integrate the solutions into their regular transactions with patrons. It can take time for everyone to get up to speed and to understand just where your patrons will need support. There are plenty of ways where eBooks are actually easier to work with for staff and patrons. With an eBook service, staff and patrons won't have to have difficult conversations about overdue fines, damaged books, lost books, or other issues related to the loaning of physical materials. It can take some time to find the right customer service balance, and for everyone to get used to the changes that can come with supporting this new collection.

SUPPORTING MULTIPLE TYPES OF DEVICES

One of the important areas where staff will need training will be to learn about all of the types of devices that your patrons are using to access eBooks. Since they may be working with patrons as they set up their devices as well as answer questions about returning eBooks or using specific device features, you won't want to underestimate training and ongoing support in this area. Even if you only plan to offer limited support of device questions, you will still get some questions from patrons about their devices; and you will need to consider how to address them.

The method you implement will vary by the size of your library or system, the number of staff you have to train, and the funding you have to purchase devices to use for training. In general, you will want to develop a device training plan that will give your staff the opportunity to get hands-on experience with a number of the devices your patrons are using, and that will let them walk through the whole process, from setting up an account to checking out and returning an eBook. And since new devices often enter the market, having a plan to update your devices periodically, and get them out into the hands of your staff, will be essential to your success.

In addition to your own in-house training, many of the eBook vendors are providing increasingly detailed online training on their website. While these training modules are often intended for patron use, they can be a great resource for staff training also. Vendors are also creating print materials that have step-by-step instructions as to how to obtain an eBook from the library and lists of frequently asked questions. Both the online materials and the written documentation are increasingly comprehensive in what they cover, and since they are aimed at the end user, they should be accessible for staff who has limited technical skills or is new to eBooks. And using these tools will give your staff a better idea of what they include and how they approach different questions, which should help when they are using these tools with patrons.

One thing to consider as you work with staff on learning about devices is just how far you plan for them to go when helping patrons with device questions. Some libraries have been offering device setup labs where patrons can bring in brand-new devices and staff will walk them through the whole process. They start from setting up their new device to getting them set up with any library software or other tools needed to access eBooks. They'll give a complete overview of device functionality and help the patron understand how their device works. On the other end of the spectrum, some libraries discourage staff from handling patron devices of any type. They direct patrons to other resources including help information and customer service from the device manufacturer. They are concerned about liability issues related to user devices, or with staff ability to provide the right level of accurate information across so many possible devices. They focus on the steps to connect patrons to library resources once the patrons have set up the device themselves. How you approach this will depend on your staff capacity, community need, and possibly any policies and practices already in place for your library. Knowing where you need your staff to be on this issue is key; they may either have to build and maintain new skills, or they will need to work within the service limitations that you have developed. As devices and eBooks access process gets easier, some of the pressures in this area are lessening. But you will always have some patrons bringing in new devices and looking for some level of assistance. You will need at least a basic framework for staff to know how to provide the appropriate level of customer service.

PUBLIC PROGRAMMING

As a way to support patrons new to eBooks, many libraries offer classes or programs for eBook users. The types of programs offered can vary quite widely, ranging from group sessions on specific types of devices to one-on-one sessions where staff meets with an individual patron to go over the eBook process, device questions, and other areas of interest for the patron. There are as many ways to provide in-person programs for the public as there are libraries, and community needs for specific types of programming or support will vary also. While offering public programming may be an important part of your library's overall service strategy, it should be evaluated regularly to make sure it's meeting the patron's actual needs.

One of the challenges related to eBook programming is tied to the frequency of changes happening in the eBook world. Curriculum and print materials need to be revised frequently and updated often. You and your staff presenting the programs need to be sure that all are staying current with changes in the devices and vendor tools. While this is also true for staff providing service to patrons at all library service points, it's especially important for staff leading public programming where patrons have been invited in to learn from staff expertise. If your library is considering offering public programming, developing a plan to ensure that high-quality, current content is provided will be an important part of making this strategy a success.

VENDOR WEBSITES AND INTEGRATIONS

Whether you have developed your own platform or are using a vendor platform, your staff will need to know how to use the platforms so they can help patrons find the books they're looking for. They'll need to know how to look for titles and subjects, how to find the Help information, how to find account information, and all of the other features of the sites you're using. If your library has integrated eBook information into your catalog, your staff will also need to know and be able to use this additional functionality.

Most vendor sites are fairly easy to use, so becoming comfortable with them should be fairly straightforward for your staff. It's important that staff members know the basic functionality of these sites because many patrons consider them an extension of the library site (if not the actual library site itself) and expect staff to know all of the ins and outs of how they work.

If you are using a vendor site, consider having the vendor provide some staff training. They may be able to do this as part of your setup process with them, or they may have other, ongoing training options. Their goal is to make it easy for your patrons to find books on their site, so helping your staff become successful using their platform is often part of the package they offer.

If you are using multiple vendors, making sure your staff understand how each of the sites work will be an important part of supporting your patrons. When patrons contact the library, they often don't know what vendor site they're using, or that you may have more than one vendor. They may ask about the search interface, or account information, and may not be able to tell you much more, and they may actually think they are on the library's own website. The more your staff members are familiar with all of the vendor tools, the quicker they'll be able to untangle the patron's question and get to the right resource.

In many ways, vendor API integration can minimize the need for additional staff training or patron support. Because the eBook information is integrated directly into your site, it's familiar to both patrons and staff. The API can minimize the need to link to the vendor website for many parts of the eBook process, since availability information, account details, and similar resources are on the library's own site. Staff still needs to understand how the process works, and some patrons will still use the vendor website also, but minimizing the transitions between vendor and library tools can make the online experience easier for your staff to support.

COLLECTION

What your staff members need to know about collection trends in eBooks may depend on what you purchase for your collection. It is good that library staff has at least a basic understanding of some of the unique issues in eBook publishing. If staff members know some of the overall trends in publishing, it will help them talk with patrons about what types of books are more likely to be available as eBooks, and why some things are more likely to be found in physical versions. They will also want to know about some of the challenges that are unique to the current state of eBook publishing. One such issue was mentioned earlier in this book. There are still some contemporary titles that are not available in an eBook version. These are titles which the copyright holder has not yet agreed to have an eBook version be published. There are other popular books, including classic titles, that are not yet available as an eBook as not all publishers are converting all of their backlists to eBooks, or doing it at a pace that meets patron demand. There still may be some series that are not completely available in eBook format which may seem odd, but often has to do with the fact that more than one publisher owns the copyright for the series. One publisher may have made the latest books in the series available digitally, but the publisher for the other beginning parts of the series has not. As the eBook market matures, there are less and less anomalies, but there will probably always be some. The best way to determine if a title you are searching for is one of the anomalies is to search online bookstore sites. If none of the major bookstores list the title in eBook format, it probably has not been published as an eBook.

A few other publishing trends would be good for library staff to know about and to be able to talk to patrons about. For instance, there are some publishers who only publish in eBook format, but their content will not be available through library vendors. Since the ability to produce an eBook is becoming easier as more people and publishers are familiar with the format, entities that are not book publishers in the traditional sense are beginning to produce eBooks. For example, some local newspapers are producing eBook content of local interest that is available for purchase only through their website. Patrons may request these types of materials and then want to know why the library doesn't have them; an informed staff will make these conversations with patrons go more smoothly.

Beyond the broader trends in publishing that affect what you can purchase, staff will need to know if there are specific patterns in what you're purchasing for your library. If you have more than one vendor, are you purchasing the same book from both of them so they're available on multiple platforms, or are you only buying certain types of titles from specific vendors? Are you not purchasing older titles, or newer titles? Are there other things about what you're purchasing that will help staff when they talk with patrons? Making sure your staff members are in the loop will help them provide better service to patrons, and hopefully minimize requests for books you're not able to purchase.

If you already have a process in place for updating your staff on trends in publishing or what you're purchasing, it's easy to start including information about eBooks in what you already do. Staff is familiar with your process already, and it puts your new eBook collection right in the middle of the broader collection conversation for your library. If you don't have a regular way to share information with staff about collection trends, you may want to consider starting something, at least as you launch your collection. As you can see, there are a number of new things to be aware of in eBook publishing that are different from what your staff and patrons are used to with print. Taking the time to make sure your staff members have current, accurate information about your new collection will help them feel connected to the change, and will also make sure your patrons are getting accurate information.

STAYING CURRENT

As you can tell, change is a constant when working with eBooks. One of the most important things you'll want to consider as you implement your collection is how you're going to help your staff stay current and connected to what's happening in your library, and with your patrons. The information you have when you launch your collection will get you started, but you'll want to make sure you're keeping everyone abreast of changes in a few key areas. Some additional information on this topic is available in Chapter 8.

One area where you'll want to make a plan to stay current relates to devices and related technology. As your patrons change devices, your staff needs to be prepared to change with them. Sometimes it's fairly easy to know when there are new devices available, since there can be very visible marketing campaigns tied to some of the new phones, tablets, and eReaders. Following mainstream media channels should be enough for you to know what's going to be available for your patrons when they're ready for a new device. While it's not possible to know all of the new options that your patrons may have, paying attention to some of the major vendors and device types should help you be prepared for changes here.

Another area that can change without much notice is related to the services provided by your vendors. As you know, vendors can change many parts of their service at any time, often with little advance notice. They can update their website, add or remove web content, or make other changes that impact the way your patrons can get their eBooks. Most of these changes are improvements, but they are still changes, and you may not know about them in advance. So while you may not always be able to prepare for these changes, you'll want to make sure you have staff actively monitoring communication from your vendors. You'll need a process in place so that you're sure that this information is shared in a timely manner with the staff members who need to know about the changes. Depending upon the size of your staff, the people who need to know could be your public service staff, your Help Desk, technical team, your collection staff, or any others who need to be aware of what happened, as they are the ones who will address any impact the change has on your patrons or staff.

In some cases these changes may need to be communicated directly to patrons. Sometimes it may be enough to make sure your staff are aware of it so they can answer any questions that may come in. At other times, you may also want your staff to follow up with the vendors to let them know how the change affected your patrons or your internal processes, in case they need to make adjustments on their end. This is seldom a perfect process. But having open communication with your vendor and a focus on supporting your patrons will help you work through any changes your vendor makes.

CHANGES IN PATRON BEHAVIOR

It may be hard to believe, but more than your devices and other tools, your patrons and their needs will be what will change the most in your environment. They'll go from being beginning eBook users who need help understanding how to get an eBook on to their new device to experienced users who expect both increasingly sophisticated help from you and increased functionality from your vendors. They'll start with one device, and then change to another one, becoming a new user again as they learn their new device. They'll learn how their new device may expand, or limit, the way they can get eBooks from the library. They may start as leisure readers, and expand their use to cookbooks and travel guides, with new expectations about what's in your collection and how eBooks work on their device. They may start to take library eBooks with them when they travel for work or leisure, and want to get help from your staff from wherever they are, not just by walking into your library.

Your patrons will also be responding to the changes going on in the broader world, and bringing some of those to you. As they increasingly use mobile devices, they'll expect you to adapt to these as well, with minimal disruption to their service. They may be getting new devices from school or work, and need new types of collection to support their projects. They will be learning new skills and tools, moving through a cycle of novice to expert and back to novice as they do; and your library staff and collections will need to be able to move with them, providing support wherever they are in the process.

This can make it an exciting time to provide a new eBook collection, since you'll be supporting your patrons as they learn new skills, and expand the ways they can use the library. But it can also be challenging, since your patrons and your staff members are continuously in a place of learning and growth, and may not feel a sense of mastery. This is where it's easy to forget that the real goal here is, at the core, to find the right book to read. Staying focused in the real reason we're all doing this work will help you stay committed to all of the components of your new eBook collection, and will help you enjoy all of the changes happening for you and your patrons.

CONNECTING BOOKS AND READERS IN THE eBOOK WORLD

When talking about eBooks, much of the conversation is about technology. You need to evaluate platforms, consider DRM, and get familiar with devices. You need to learn about file types, download options, and digital literacy. It's easy to forget that the reason you're doing all of this work is to get books into the hands of your library patrons. While eBooks may bring a lot of new tools and technology to the table, at the core, they're just a new way to provide a long-standing library service.

So, how do you plan to provide that traditional service of getting books into the hands of patrons in this new way? How does your eBook collection align with the way you're currently providing this service to your patrons? How will you need to adjust what you do to connect with your patrons in this new way? As you roll out your new collection, you'll want to take some time to explore how you're going to connect your eBooks to your broader service for readers.

When a patron asks you for a book for a research project, or to take on vacation, it's easy to forget to offer him or her all of the formats you have available. But many of your patrons would be just as happy with an eBook as they would with a print copy. Their request is format-neutral. They just want a copy of the book for their Book Club next week, or need something they can take home today to use for their history paper. They may not know you have eBooks, so they may not ask for them specifically. They're working with your staff, or checking your online catalog, looking for a book, the same as your patrons have done for years. Now they just have one more way to do that. This is one of the ways where the service you offer your patrons doesn't change when you add eBooks. Just as you'd make sure that you'd offer an audiobook version to a patron looking for a copy of a book for a Book Club, you'd offer an eBook also. It can be a little more difficult since you can't just walk over the physical shelf to see what's checked in. You need to remember that you can browse your online shelves as well to meet the patrons need. Then again, the patron may not be interested in an eBook, just as they may not be interested in an audiobook. An eBook or audiobook might not meet their need for this specific request, or they might not have the devices needed to use those formats. But making sure that all formats are available for a patron to select from is the standard way we make our collections available, and adding eBooks is just one more way for a patron to get the book he or she needs.

It's also important to remember that, regardless of the packaging, a good book is still a good book. Your patrons are looking for a new cookbook to use for a party, or something to take their mind off a health issue. *War and Peace* is still *War and Peace* whether it's in paperback or EPUB version. People go through the "hassle" of the device/vendor challenges because they want the story, or the information they're looking for. Your role is to make the connection to the right book for the reader. It's easy to start with the device and format questions, and lose track of the real reason the patron is using the library. Your goal is to help patrons get the best from your collections, making sure they know what's available, and what aligns with their reading or research interests. If they're looking for a cozy mystery, or a history book about a specific time period, then you want to make sure that you understand what they're looking for and connect them to the best options you have. One of the challenges is that your eBook collection is likely to be smaller and less comprehensive than your print collection, and that may always be the case. You may have fewer options to provide if your patron only wants an eBook and isn't interested in what's in your physical collection. This is where your advisory services and support can become a little more complicated. For instance, if you're not purchasing much nonfiction for your eBook collection, it will be more difficult to meet your patrons' needs when they're looking for a selection of nonfiction, and want to read only in the eBook format. You experience this with your print collections also. You still have limits to what you purchase in physical formats, but your collection is probably much larger and deeper in print. In addition, you may have access to inter-library loan for physical items not in your collection. Understanding what your patron is looking for, and knowing what's available in your eBook collection that can meet that need, is similar to what we already do with our other collections. Your eBook collection may operate a little differently, but at the very basic level, you're trying to meet the patron's need with the collection you have. You start with a focus on the book itself, and not the technology needed to get to it, and this focus will help you make a better connection to the reader.

However, connecting eBooks and readers has some different challenges also. In many ways, eBooks advisory is comparable to audiobooks advisory, where the reading experience is "enhanced" by the person reading the audiobook. While the words are the same across all the formats the book can be available in, the narrator of the audiobook adds an additional level of complexity to the advisory process. The same types of additional complexity happen with eBooks. While the book is still the book, there are some additional levels to the advisory process that need to be considered.

In addition, some eBooks and some devices have features that change or enhance the experience. There are eBooks that include in-text links to maps, and other materials provide additional resources for the reader, and that make the book the same, and yet different from the print version of the same book. In addition, some devices provide bookmarking and highlighting functionality and include dictionaries and similar reference materials. Some also have text-to-voice functionality that essentially turns the eBook into an audiobook.

While a book is a book is a book, sometimes there are additional things that need to be taken into consideration. Is your patron looking at history or travel books where additional maps in the eBook version make it a better choice? Does your patrons' device have text-to-voice, so they could listen to it on a road trip since there's no audiobook version available? Your patrons are still looking for the right book to fit their needs, but the eBook version may add some additional options.

To make sure you're reaching your patrons with relevant information about your eBook collection, you'll want to understand where your patrons are finding out about what you have available for them. Since many people who read eBooks are willing to read a book in any format, they may not come to your library or go to your website looking for an eBook. They may not go to your vendor website or check out your locally developed platform to see what books are there. They'll be looking for books the way they always have: checking your catalog and online booklists, browsing the shelves of your library, checking out displays, or talking with your staff. They may be looking for a book their friends told them about, or they may be looking for books on gardening. You'll want to make sure you're finding your readers where they are, especially since your eBooks won't be "visible" to them on your shelves or displays.

To make sure you're reaching your patrons, you'll want to evaluate the ways they could connect with this part of your collection. If you want to make sure your eBooks get the same type of exposure you provide the rest of your collection, you'll want to review all of the ways you connect with your patrons, in-library and online, to make sure you've integrated your new collection into your broader service strategy. In addition to the marketing and promotional planning ideas mentioned in Chapter 4, you also have opportunities for connection and promotion through your eBook website.

For lots of your users, your vendors' website may be a primary way they learn about what eBooks you have available. Vendors increasingly allow libraries to customize their websites, creating display shelves and other features that appeal to readers. While it's possible to have these types of lists populated by the vendor, you may want to consider having your staff curate these also. It will allow you to align your eBook lists with other types of lists or displays you may have in your buildings, create lists of local interest for your community, or create lists especially designed for your identified target audiences. If this is where your patrons are finding books, you need to make sure you're investing time to make sure those patrons are getting a good experience.

Your patrons are also probably looking for books in your catalog and on your website. You'll want to make sure you've included your eBooks on any relevant online lists, and looked into adding new lists that highlight your eBooks if possible as well.

Since your catalog is the primary way your patrons expect to find the books in your collection, you'll definitely want to review the way your eBooks are presented there. This is especially true if you have more than one eBook vendor, or if you've developed your own platform. You'll want to make sure that it's easy for your patrons to identify which format they're selecting, and to see the file types that are available. With multiple vendors or other issues, you'll want to provide as much detail as possible to help users determine that the book they're selecting is the right one for their device. But the technical details aren't the only things of interest to your eBook readers. If you have cover art, reviews, or other reader-friendly content for your print materials, you'll want to make sure you have the same coverage for your eBooks. While there are a lot of small details to consider here, they will help ensure that your eBook patrons have the same experience as your print readers, and that they can find the same type of information about the books they're interested in.

Making sure that your patrons know about your eBook collection, and can find the books they're interested in where they would expect to find them, is an important part of making sure that you're reaching them and meeting their service need. eBooks bring some unique challenges for connecting with readers, but some great opportunities also. Taking the time to make sure your long-standing support for readers and information-seekers also supports the eBook format will contribute to the success of your service.

CONCLUSION

Launching a new eBook collection can be exciting. Adding a new collection, and expanding access to your library services, can help you connect in new ways with your current users, as well as expand your reach to new users. While it's important to focus on the collection and the technical issues related to a new or expanded eBook collection, taking the time to plan how you'll promote your new collection, engage your staff, and make the connection to the wider range of services that your library offers is an important part of the overall success of your initiative.

Our library supports patron use of eBooks and eReaders by:
- Providing public support and training in person, by phone, and online (including direct patron support by library staff, and with resources provided by vendors, as well as limited library-created content)
- Providing training content that can be reused, focusing on one-to-many service, and developing tools that patrons can use independently as well as that staff can share with patrons
- Supporting 24/7 access to training content

Classes for the public will be led by designated library staff, and will be developed in collaboration with departments, communities organizations, and so on.

Print materials (handouts, posters, etc.) should be created by designated library staff or in collaboration with eBook planning team, Communication or Marketing Department, and so on.

Figure 5.1 Library Support for eBooks and eReaders

Questions on which devices to purchase are Reference, Readers Advisory, or Technical/Help Desk questions. Staff should direct patrons to standard consumer resources for basic information and to vendor-provided resources for information about which devices are compatible with library collections.

Patrons with questions related to their own computers/devices may be asking Reference or Readers Advisory or Technical/Help Desk questions, depending on the level of detail needed.

Staff are expected to be familiar with the support and training resources available to the public by:
- Reviewing the information provided on the public website
- Being familiar with basic circulation policies related to downloadable materials (loan periods, library card policies, etc.)
- Using library-provided devices for hands-on training
- Attending in-person and online training in this area

Our library is focused on access to content: books, music, and movies.
- We will focus on the long-term, supporting patron access to downloadable collections and content, and sustainable service.

Our library will (or will not) pursue lending devices.
- Devices are rapidly changing technology, and individual devices become outdated quickly.
- Lending devices are potentially a violation of the Terms of Service of most devices, and so would not be supported.

Figure 5.1 (Continued)

CHAPTER 6

Evaluating the Success of Your New Collection

When adding or changing any service, you want to be able to evaluate whether your strategy is successful, and whether your financial investment has an impact for your patrons. As you move ahead with your eBook collection, you should establish several areas where you want to measure the changes: your budget, your access points, and your services. While each of these may require some different measurement tools, developing a comprehensive approach as to what you plan to measure as part of your launch plan will help you start as you mean to go on. Having an evaluation plan in place will help guide your future growth.

BUDGET

To get started with your eBook collection, you would have needed to allocate funding to purchase your start-up collection. Those funds may have come from savings in other areas of your budget, one-time start-up funds, or from other funding sources. You'll want to consider your overall eBook budget allocation as part of your overall budget strategy, regardless of the size of your budget. However you allocated the funding to get started, you'll want to be prepared to measure your expenditures against your budget to help determine your next steps. As you've seen in earlier chapters, the eBook purchasing process can be complicated, and there are multiple purchasing models at play. This makes the overall budgeting process for eBooks complicated. You'll want to spend time to understand how the eBook purchasing models will have an impact on your overall budget. If you're planning to expand your collection, you will need to know how you will budget with so many purchasing variables.

One obvious indicator of success is when the demands for eBook purchases outstrip the budget you have allocated. When that happens, it is important to step back and reaffirm your intentions and then your message to your stakeholders. Spending your allocated funds quickly and completely may mean that you need to increase your funding for eBooks going forward, but that theory will need to be validated against actual patron use data. It can be easy to spend your allocated budget right away, since there will be many more books of interest than you have funding available. But spending your budget quickly doesn't necessarily mean you need to immediately allocate more funding, especially if your use indicators don't show that the books you've purchased are being used, or being used at the level you'd projected. It could instead mean that your budget allocation is the right size, but your purchasing plan or your promotion and marketing plan needs to be adjusted to maximize the funding you've already allocated. If patrons aren't checking out what you purchased, or aren't using the collection at a level that aligns with your overall goals, a budget increase may not be warranted at this point, even if you've spent all your funding. You'll want to watch what's happening in terms of patron use, especially if increasing your eBook budget will mean decreasing funding in other collection areas or decreasing what you can offer in terms of service.

If your eBook collection funding is part of your overall collection budget, you'll want to evaluate your spending for eBooks with the same criteria you do for other parts of your collection. You may already have some framework in place for this with other formats. If that's the case, you should be able to just extend the framework for print, audiobooks, and other areas to your eBook collection. Doing so would allow you to maintain a consistent approach across all parts of your collection, making it easier to evaluate all parts of your budget with the same criteria. Or, with the addition of this new collection, you may need to re-evaluate your process, to make sure it can support the addition of another new way to purchase materials.

Some things to consider as you start reviewing the budget you've allocated for eBooks include evaluating any expectations or benchmarks. These benchmarks could be dollars expended per circulation or overall percentage of budget allocated to nonprint materials, overall percentage allocated to children's materials regardless of format, and so on. Many libraries have some general benchmarks or baseline standards they use to allocate funding. Whatever method you use at your library will need to be adjusted to include this new collection. If, in general, you allocate 50% of your collection budget for children's materials, perhaps this means you want 50% of your eBook budget to be allocated this way as well. You will need to determine how your actual use data combines with other marketplace factors. Even if you want to have an even split between children's and adult titles in eBook form, you may not be able to achieve that goal. It could be that there aren't as many eBooks available to purchase for children as there are for adults, or that you find children in your service area use print more than they use eBooks.

Or if you allocate 25% of your overall fiction collection budget to romance, and so use that same guideline for eBooks, you may find that your eBook titles are always checked out and have waiting lists, and you're getting patron comments about the small size of your collection. Your romance eBook collection could be used at a higher rate than your print collection, which may lead you to consider adjusting your budget allocation, or your guidelines for purchasing materials. As your patrons start using your collection, you will need to evaluate which materials they're actually checking out and determine where you need to adjust, or expand, your funding.

In many cases eBook copies are not a "new" title; they're yet another way to buy copies of titles you may already have in print, as an audiobook, and so on. By adding yet another format, you may find your library purchasing even fewer overall titles, since you're purchasing more versions of a smaller number of titles. This is also something you'll want to watch, especially if you're working with multiple eBook vendors. You may find that eBooks have an unexpected impact on your overall collection budget. If you're now purchasing a smaller number of titles overall, it could be an area where you set some preliminary guidelines or benchmarks for purchasing to see if this is going to become an issue that needs additional review for your library. It may take a while for you to be able to see what's happening in this area and what impact it may have on your selection process and budget, but it's definitely an area to watch for, and to be prepared to evaluate.

There are some places in your budget where you should expect to see some cost savings by moving to eBooks. Since eBooks are digital materials, they don't need spine labels, genre stickers, barcodes, ownership markings, security or RFID tags, lamination, plastic CD or audiobook cases, or bindery repair. And if you are paying for eBook cataloging from another vendor, this too may be less expensive than the cost of in-house cataloging. As you launch or expand your eBook collection, especially if you are shifting funds from physical materials to eBooks, you should also see decreases in the need for these types of supplies and/or value-added services. Depending on the size of your collection and the types of materials you purchase these may not be a huge cost saving. However, you should be able to realize at least some small savings here, and this may offset part of the expenses of launching a new collection.

Another area to watch as a budget measure is the impact the move to eBooks could have on your fine revenue. Of course, not all libraries assess fines on overdue, damaged, or lost materials. If your library doesn't collect fines and fees, then eBooks should have no impact in this area for you. However, if your library does charge fees for materials that come back late, you may see a decrease in funds collected as patrons start using your eBooks. Since eBooks either "expire" (DRM formats) or stay with the user (DRM-free formats), they are never late, lost, or damaged, and so don't accrue fees. The impact on your library will vary based on how much fine and fee revenue you usually collect each year, what happens with those funds, and how much of a decrease you'll see from patrons moving to eBooks. Your situation will be unique to your library, but be prepared to discuss with your stakeholders the loss of fine revenue, especially if the loss has an impact on your library budget or other funding streams. Of course, since you are not assessing fines or fees for these materials, you do not have to allocate staff time to work with patrons on fine collection issues, or to process the financial paperwork needed to support fines and fees. While this may not lead to an easily measurable cost savings in staff time, it should free up some staff time for other tasks.

CIRCULATION

If your patrons enthusiastically embrace eBooks, it is easy to be awed by the often double-digit increases in circulation that come when you launch your new collection or expand it with an infusion of new titles. The increases can be impressive, and it's easy to assume that this is the trajectory they will take going forward, even if you know that realistically this can't be the case.

Circulation of materials is one of the standard ways libraries measure activity and patron use. It's a measurement that your administration and stakeholders are used to seeing, and that your staff is used to using for purchasing materials and designing services. With this in mind, you already know that it is important to look at where and how eBook circulation fits into the overall circulation of your library or library system. It's a measure that your library will be looking for as a primary way to evaluate the success of your collection, even if it's a measure that may not tell the whole story of what's happening, especially as you're getting started.

As an example, perhaps you start an eBook collection and within a year you see exponential increases in eBook circulation month to month. No other collection is showing that type of growth, so it is natural to want to continue to support that growth by allocating additional funding, or moving funding away from lower-growth collections. After another year, your eBook circulation is now perhaps 20% of your total circulation. That is tremendous growth in a short amount of time. eBook circulation may even be one of the major factors in an overall increase in circulation for your library. Before making drastic changes in what you purchase, however, it is important to put eBook circulation in the context of your whole circulation package. Using our example, 20% of circulation may now be coming from eBooks, but it follows that 80% of your circulation is coming from the rest of your collection. You don't want to ignore or downplay your 80%, especially if your overall collection budget isn't increasing. You want to continue to grow your popular collection, but if you make drastic changes, you can end up compromising the breadth and depth of your overall collection, where the majority of your circulation remains.

This type of situation does give you yet another chance to look at your budget allocations. Staying with our example, are you spending 20% of your budget on eBooks? Are you above or below that percentage? Does your budget allocation line up with your overall circulation, or is there some alignment to do there? Of course, not all types of materials cost the same, so using a straight percentage is a simplistic example. Just as a hardcover "coffee-table" book of photos may cost more than a mass market paperback, so an eBook version of a popular novel may cost more than a print version of the same book depending on the purchasing model. The same budget allocation may purchase a larger or smaller number of books, based on what's being purchased, which then leads to the potential higher or lower circulation in different areas with the same allocated funding. But thinking through your allocations and your reasoning for your allocations allows you to have ready answers for your stakeholders when they ask about your eBook circulation and how it's aligning with other parts of your collection. You can also respond as to how an increase or decrease in funding may impact circulation.

In previous chapters it was mentioned that the way publishers assign the subject heading or age level of a book may not be the same as the way your library has classed or classified the physical book. Depending on what you purchase and how you classify materials, this disconnect can make comparing circulation between physical and eBook copies tricky, especially if you choose not to have your staff adjust the eBook records to match your records for other parts of your collection. For example, your library may have deemed a certain title as most appropriate for an adult audience. A publisher, on the other hand, has decided that it wants to market the title more for a young adult audience and has labeled the title as teen. While this may not make a significant difference in your overall measures, it's a reminder that you may not be comparing the same things. The difference can become significant when you are purchasing heavily in certain areas and there are enough differences in audience between your physical collection and eBook collection to start showing up in your circulation figures or measure of general collection size. This is something to watch for, especially if you begin to see your eBook and physical collections varying widely in circulation. It could be because your patrons are using your eBooks and physical collections differently. But it could also be because a few popular titles with multiple copies are measured as "adult" in your print collection and as "teen" in your eBook collection.

Your ability to evaluate your eBook circulation may also be dependent on what reports are available from your vendors or from the system you have developed locally. It's likely that the information you receive will not match with the reporting you use from your integrated library system (ILS) for your physical collection, especially if you are using vendor reporting tools. Vendor reports are ideally something you should understand, at least at a basic level, as you launch your collection. To make sure you understand where your vendor reports align with your other collection reporting and where they may differ, you'll want to take the time to review your reporting options and understand what your vendor is able to provide. Asking your vendors to explain what's included and is not included in their reporting tools is key to knowing what reports you can use to compare to information from your ILS and what reports will differ. Even with reporting limitations, there is certainly important information to be gleaned from analysis of your eBook collection in comparison to your physical collection. This is an area where you can expect staff, stakeholder, and potentially patron and media questions. Knowing what's possible to provide and where there may be gaps will help you tell the most accurate story you can about your eBook circulation.

One approach to get started would be to start with a birds-eye view and then slowly dig deeper to see what you can glean. Start by answering a broad question about your collection, looking at comparisons between adult and children's materials, or between eBooks, audiobooks, and print. Identify a few key areas to start with to see what you can learn at the macro level of your collection. This will let you see some of larger trends that may be happening, especially as you're able to track your circulation data over a longer period of time.

As you start reviewing the information you've been able to collect, ask yourself, "why do we think the results are the way they are?" List any circumstances you think might have a bearing on the numbers you have. While one assumption is that you've selected the right books for your audience, it's possible that there are other, additional things going on that are having an effect on circulation, either for eBooks or for your collection as a whole. For example, perhaps you opened a library branch devoted to children's material and services in the past year. You would expect that your circulation for children's material would be increasing, and that would lead to an overall increase in these materials that could be unrelated to the launch of your eBook collection. Maybe you had an initiative to provide library cards to all of the students in your community, and brought them all to the library for tours. You'd hopefully see an increase in circulation in a few areas there also. Your library card initiative could lead to an increase in eBook circulation, but simply adding eBooks wasn't what led to the increase. Statistics have a narrative and a story. It's always a good idea to track what's happening in your broader story when you're asked at a future date why the numbers were the way they were. Then you will have the relevant context and background at your fingertips. Sometimes increases or decreases happen for reasons you can't fully explain, but there are many changes that are tied to things you can control, or at least impact; and you'll want to track those areas carefully. Like opening a new building or a library card initiative, you may be trying to make an impact in several areas at once and it's easy to forget how the launch of an eBook collection may be affected by other initiatives or policy changes.

As you come to better understand your data, the next series of questions you ask might take you to a more granular level of detail. For example: within adult materials, do fiction or nonfiction materials circulate more? Are these trends similar in print and eBooks, or are they different? Again, you'll want to make note of any underlying circumstances that would have a bearing on the numbers. This next level of detail will take you to a deeper level of collection use, and a place where you may actually be able to see more differences in how your patrons are using your collections differently.

Going one step further, consider where your information about your physical collection and your eBook collection may start to diverge. Generally, a larger library system will most likely agree with vendors and publishers as to whether a book is fiction or nonfiction. But you may have differences of opinion on what type a fiction or nonfiction book is. Is this fiction title a romance or is it a thriller? Is this nonfiction book about a specific sport, or a biography of a famous athlete? This is where you'll want to be aware of what percentage of your titles may differ in how they're classified between your collection types, especially if you're using breakdowns within one collection that aren't available for the other. It may not be a meaningful difference for your collection, or you may have some work to do to be able to compare and contrast your circulation across the different platforms. This is also where it's good to start looking at your collections by subject or genre: cookbooks, travel, mystery, and others.

Going one step deeper can give you further insight into trends in circulation. Looking at the performance of a selection of specific titles, focusing on those that you have both in physical versions and eBook versions can give you information on whether your patrons have a format preference for a specific type of subject, and whether you and the vendor are agreeing on how the titles are classified and therefore how they are being counted. Obviously, you can't do this for all titles, but sampling some of the titles on a regular basis will give you an idea as to how much you can rely on the vendor reports to align with the reports on your physical collection. If the difference in how a vendor counts and how you count is close enough by your standards, then you can use vendor reports with confidence to analyze how your eBook collection is being used in comparison to your physical collection.

By doing this analysis, you gain the opportunity to tailor your collections to your patrons' needs and wants. You'll be able to see trends at a high level, as well as develop format preferences in specific types of materials or parts of your collections. Giving your patrons more of what they need and want is definitely a measure of success, and understanding and using your circulation data will help you meet that goal.

MEASURING WEB AND ONLINE ACCESS

While circulation may be a better way to measure patron use than hits on your website, you will also want to be aware of the way patrons are accessing your eBooks, and be prepared to speak to what this means for your overall use. Website hits may also help you understand patron behavior, and help you track unexpected changes in your online statistics that may come from your new or expanded collection.

In general, libraries track website users or sessions as a way to demonstrate that patrons are using the library website, and to understand what they are doing once they are on the website. If you are using a vendor-provided platform to provide your eBooks, your patrons are likely to come to your website, then click through the site to get to the vendor website, giving you measurable web statistics. They may bypass your main page and bookmark your eBook landing page, but they'll still be tracked in your overall website use statistics. That won't tell you how many unique patrons are doing this, or how many books they check out once they get there, but it will give you an idea of how many patrons are taking that path.

Your patrons may have other ways to get their eBooks, however. They may be able to get to the vendor website directly, or may also use the separate apps provided by the vendor. In both of those cases, patrons are not using your library website, and so are not showing up in your web statistics. Depending on what you've been tracking, and if patrons are switching how they access eBooks, this may lead to a decline in your overall web use statistics, since patrons are now going directly to the vendor access points. For your patrons, this may be an improved service. Using the vendor app directly on their devices may be the best way to get their books, but it may lead to a shift in your broader use statistics. While knowing how many patrons have downloaded the vendor app may seem like a useful statistic, it doesn't really tell you anything about use or activity. It's a one-time action that doesn't tell you if your patrons actually use the app, or if they are using it to check out or read eBooks. It may be a piece of the puzzle, but you should be looking for more action-based statistics to truly understand what your patrons are doing.

If you are interested in learning more about how your patrons are using your vendor websites and apps, you will want to talk with your vendors about what types of statistics they're able to provide for you. Do they have web analytics for their website that they can share? Can they provide reports as to how many active patrons are using your collection? How many "new" patrons have set up accounts in order to use the service? Web analytics may help you see if patrons are browsing their site and looking for reading suggestions, or if they're primarily looking for titles they're already aware of. That type of information will help you better understand your users, and is important for you to be aware of even if your patrons are using the vendor website and not your website or catalog to select their titles. You may also be able to run web analytics yourself on your vendor website. However you approach this, it's worth exploring your options if your patrons are using both your vendor website and apps to do their eBook requests and selection.

Watching reports on number of active patrons month per month may give you an insight into the success of your promotional material and the success the contents of your collection. If you begin to see a decline in active users over time, it may be an indication that you need to do some more analysis to determine the causes. It could be that your regular users have read everything in your collection that's of interest and you need to increase your collection. Or perhaps they've shifted their reading behavior and they're no longer reading as many eBooks and have moved back to print. New patron data may have more of an impact in the first months after launch, when all of your patrons will be considered "new" as they set up accounts to access your collection. At some point, just as with library cards, you may end up saturating your service area and this data becomes less useful. However, if you stop getting any new patrons for several weeks or months, you may want to evaluate your promotion and marketing plan, or talk with your patrons about what else may be keeping new patrons from trying out this part of your collection.

Your vendors have a stake in seeing your eBook service succeed, because more demand from your patrons will most likely lead to more sales for them. Ask your vendor(s) how they are interpreting the use of your collection, and what they're seeing in comparison with libraries that are similar in service area or collection size to yours. Remember because this data is living in their system, they have access to it as well, and are often willing to share at least some of the high-level information with you. You'll be able to make your own interpretations based on what you see with any data they can provide you. But as eBook vendors grow their businesses, they are most likely devoting more resources to analyzing library use data than you are, and it would be good to include their perspective and insights into the data you've been able to collect.

If you are developing your own platform, you'll want to consider how you will measure use, and what functionality you'll need to build or include in your staff tools. Will you be tracking circulation, or also using web analytics or other measures to see how many patrons are using your online platform? While your answers may vary depending on how you set up your site, you'll definitely want to consider if, or how, you'll be measuring online use, especially as it aligns with other online resources and general circulation that you already report. Since this is a platform you'll be developing and managing, you'll want to make sure you develop and implement a clear process for evaluating both your platform and the way your patrons are using it.

MEASURING DEVICE USE

As talked about throughout this book, one of the most appealing things about eBooks is that they can be read on many types of devices. They can be accessed on desktop and laptop computers, dedicated eReaders, tablets, and smartphones. Some patrons may read consistently from one type of device, while others may read across several types of devices as they move from home, work, and other locations. Having an understanding of what types of devices your patrons are using can help determine what formats to purchase, and how best to train your staff to support your patrons with any questions they have as they use your collection. Most eBook vendors offer eBooks in a variety of formats, ranging from PDFs to proprietary formats that work only on specific devices like the Kindle or Nook, so knowing what devices your patrons are using can help you maximize your collection expenditures and staff support.

As was first mentioned in Chapter 1, asking patrons directly about their preferences is best when you have the opportunity to do so. If you are just getting started with eBooks, you may want to start with surveying your patrons about how they expect to access your collection. Will any of them be reading on their computers? Do they plan to use a tablet, or a dedicated eReader? Even if this is just projected use, it may help you with vendor selection as well as with determining which types of formats to start with. If you are interested in surveying your patrons, see the sample survey at the end of Chapter 1 (Figure 1.1) for ideas.

Once your patrons begin using your collection, you'll want to continue to monitor what types of devices your patrons are using. Devices are changing all the time; new models come on the market with new features and functionality, and patrons who started with dedicated eReaders may move to tablets, or vice versa. Of course, many patrons keep their devices for a long time. They may not be getting new devices; they may be using older versions, so you'll want to know that also as you make your collection and staff support decisions. While this device flexibility can be great for users, it can be tricky for libraries to manage, since the decision about what device to use rests solely with the patrons, and is driven by what's happening in the broader marketplace. It would be easier for you to manage and support a smaller number of device types. You and library staff would then only need to be able to answer patron questions about a few specific devices instead of needing at least a basic understanding of a wide range of old and new models. Tracking what's happening with the devices your patrons are using will help you keep a handle on the impact this component of eBook delivery is having on your service.

If you are using a vendor-based service, you will also want to monitor their news and announcements for any changes about what devices they are supporting. Currently vendors are prepared to support most, if not all, of the newest devices. At some point, vendors may make the decision to stop supporting certain older devices, even if you still have patrons who use them to get eBooks from your library. If a vendor does make a change, you'll want to make sure all your staff members who work with your eBook service to know about the change. They will need to know the implications it may have for your service, and how best they can serve the affected patrons. Knowing even an estimate of how many of your patrons may be affected by a change in support for a specific type of device will help you manage the change, and potentially how it may impact other parts of your service. This is another way that supporting eBooks can differ from what you've needed to do with your physical collections. It's an aspect where you'll want to consider the type of customer service and messaging you're going to provide if your vendor is no longer able to support devices used by members of your community.

Of course, the types of devices that patrons use are not something you can control, so it's a different sort of thing for you to measure. An increase in the use of one type of device and a decrease in another may be almost entirely tied to changes happening outside the library. However, not watching those trends may have an impact on your patrons' overall ability to use your collection. If you purchase formats that they can't use on their devices, you may not be able to increase your circulation, and may even see a decline. Knowing that most of your patrons have devices that use EPUB may let you minimize purchases for proprietary formats like AZW, making sure that most of your patrons have access to most of the titles you've purchased for them.

CUSTOMER SERVICE

As is talked about throughout this book, your eBook collection doesn't exist in isolation from your broader collection, or from your overall services for readers of all ages. As you identify the ways you will evaluate your eBook service, you will want to make sure you are using the same methods in this area as you already use to evaluate your services for print readers. You may decide to add some new components as well, but at a minimum, you've just added a new format to your existing service, and the baseline evaluation process you already have in place should be enough to get you started.

While the way libraries measure Readers Advisory and Reference services can vary widely, it is important to have at least some basic measures in place in this area to fully understand how you are reaching eBook readers so you are able to manage, and improve, your service. Do you currently measure the number of books checked out from a display in a library building? Then consider tracking the number of books checked out from an online list or display. Do you track summer reading or book club use? Ask which patrons participating in those programs read eBooks, and be prepared to adjust your services to align with what you're hearing from them. There will be ways to include your eBooks in your current service evaluation measures, and you may find some new ways to track your services for readers as you think about how eBook readers are connecting with you.

Program attendance and program support may also be part of eBook story. If you are offering programs to patrons on how to use your library's eBook collection, how to get started with a new eReader device, or similar programs, then you'll want to have a plan in place to evaluate these programs with direct ties to your eBook initiative. In addition to the basic data you may already track about program attendance, you may want to consider asking some outcome-based questions. It's important to know how many people attend the program and possibly their age range or other key information. You will also want to know if the program met their expectations, had the right level of technical detail, provided the type of information they needed to answer their questions, and made them feel like they could go home and get a library eBook onto their own device. In addition, you may want to track the amount of staff time needed to prepare for and present these programs, since keeping up to speed on all that's needed for this type of program may take an unexpected amount of staff resources. Balancing the amount of staff time and effort needed to create and offer the programs with the expected outcomes will be an important part of your evaluation.

Just as it's important to remember to connect patrons with the "hidden" electronic collections when staff is walking through the shelves with a patron, the same is true for remembering these collections when planning public programming. If your library is offering a program about books or reading, it is important to look for the impact that program has on the eBook collection. An author talk, a community-wide book discussion, and library-led book clubs are all examples of book-based programs, where it might be easy to overlook the impact that the program has on the eBook collection. Libraries have so much experience with the physical-based collections with these types of programs. You know how to purchase additional physical copies in advance of a program as well as evaluate circulation and holds placed before and after the program has taken place. It's easy to forget some of these steps with eBooks, especially since the selection process may be different or the use data may not be in the same place. Because it's still easy to overlook effect a program has on the e-versions, try to make sure you are including these new formats in your post program evaluation.

Any marketing you set up within the vendor's website will also be important to measure. As mentioned, vendors will supply tools to market your eBook collection, including the ability to create lists or bookshelves to organize or display your titles. You may also be able to create special spaces or pages within the vendor site targeting specific age groups, allowing you to break out materials for adults, teens, and children and making it easier to promote these materials to the best audiences. As you put staff time into developing these types of tools on your vendor site, you'll want to establish a way to measure if they are reaching their intended audiences in the ways that you'd intended. While it may be easy to implement these types of features, you may discover that your patrons don't use them. On the other hand, you may find that your patrons are using them continually to browse your collection, and therefore they are definitely worth the time and energy to develop and maintain.

Anytime you are looking to promote or expand your service and implement any marketing strategies, make sure you have a measurement plan in place to evaluate the success of your initiative. While many of the ways we reach library patrons in general will also reach eBook readers, there may be some differences also. Since your eBook readers don't need to come into your building to get their books, you may need to look into new ways to reach them, and you'll want to make sure you have a plan in place to see if that's working as you intended. This can include measuring usage changes in eBooks after a promotional push, or number of handouts distributed at community events. Any measure you already have in place for measuring your services and promotions should be expanded to include your eBook collection.

You may also want to develop an ongoing, low-key process to bring in patron feedback and input into your planning. Doing regular surveys, similar to what you did when launching your collection, would be a consistent way to track trends in patron interests with minimal disruption to your service. You could target the survey to specific collection areas you're looking to expand, or other areas that need attention. Some sample surveys are included at the end of this chapter, Figure 6.1, Figure 6.2, and Figure 6.3.

WHAT DOES YOUR DATA MEAN?

While it may be helpful to review and evaluate your eBook statistics and other measures solely as a reflection of that service, eBooks are best evaluated in the broader context of your overall collection budget and service strategy. As talked about before, in one sense eBooks are just another format libraries are now offering. Most of your eBook readers probably don't read only eBooks. Depending on their circumstances, the topic they're interested in, the specific title, and availability of the title are all decision points where a patron may choose an eBook over a physical version or vice versa. Since eBook readers are using other parts of your collection as well, any changing behavior regarding their use of the rest of the collection needs to be factored into your collection evaluation. Likewise, your patrons use your library's Readers Advisory and Reference and related services to learn about all types of things to read, and for their homework or other information needs. They'll still want to know about all your other services related to Reader's Advisory and Reference, not just about eBooks.

When you're laying out any of your evaluation processes, continue to look for ways to integrate the data and other feedback you're collecting from eBooks into the broader plans you already have in place. While you definitely want to see use of your eBook collection grow, you'll want to be able to see that growth in the context of your overall goals. In terms of collection statistics, add in what you are finding in terms of circulation as we discussed earlier in this chapter by looking at such questions as: is eBook circulation growing faster or more slowly than other circulation? Is adult eBook circulation growing faster than adult print, but is children's eBook circulation increasing less quickly than children's print? By laying out what you want to, and are able to, collect about your eBook collection next to what you already have in place for your other collections and services, you'll be able to see the whole story more easily from the beginning.

As you build and expand your collection, you'll want to make sure you're looking at both short-term and longer-term changes in the data. Short-term changes are interesting, and it can often be exciting to see rapid growth on a month-to-month basis. This is especially true when you're starting a new collection, increasing your budget allocation, adding a new vendor, or launching a new marketing campaign. You'd certainly hope to see measurable increases when you make these types of changes, and reviewing them on a daily, weekly, or monthly level is a great way to monitor what's happening and make minor adjustments to your process.

However, generally library circulation and other use is seasonal. Some types of use are tied to the academic calendar, and others are tied to general trends in work and vacations and holidays. While the timing of all of these may vary by the community you're serving, you know the rhythms and use patterns of your patrons. You'll want to review the use of your eBook collection in light of what you know and expect in your broader usage trends. If your adult fiction use tends to go up in the summer because of vacations and then back down in the fall when work and school schedules pick up again, then you'll want to take a longer-term look at your use. Compare June this year to June last year, since those are months you would expect to see similar types of use, and hopefully an increase over the previous year. Comparing August this year to September this year may show a decrease and lead to questions and concerns about decreasing circulation if you just look at month-to-month numbers, when, in fact, that's part of a broader seasonal trend that you can see more clearly if you take a longer view.

As you move through launching your collection and start integrating it into your broader service strategy, you'll have more information to build on and will get a better idea of what's meaningful to track here, and what's less helpful. Taking this longer-term view will also help you see where your eBook users are similar to your broader use, and where they may be different. Are the seasonal trends you're used to seeing the same, or are they varying more (or less) throughout the year? If you live in a colder climate, does eBook use stay the same or does it increase in the winter, since patrons don't need to drive to the library on a snowy day to pick up their books? There's plenty to learn here as you start building your data and taking a longer look at what's happening.

WHAT IS THE STORY FOR YOUR STAKEHOLDERS?

Many of the statistics and other measures you'll develop as you implement your eBook collection will be used by you and your staff to manage the collection and service. You'll have budget allocations, circulation and online use, and other measures to use in your daily work with your eBooks. But while you're developing and using these measures, you'll want to make sure you're in conversation with your stakeholders. It is particularly important to stay in conversation with your director and other administrators, your library board, and others who have a vested interest in how patrons are using this collection and how it is (or isn't) having an impact on your other services.

While these audiences may be interested in the same measures you're using to manage your eBook collection, there may be other areas or types of information they want to have as well. As you're planning for your new or expanded collection, or adding new vendors, make sure you understand what will be important to your stakeholders so you're prepared to address any questions or concerns that may arise.

Start by talking with them about their level of interest and understanding of eBooks and the related collection, technical and service issues. What information is relevant to them? What do they need to be able to speak about eBooks with the audiences they work or interact with? These audiences could be funders, community members, and others. You may need to help tailor the message to stakeholders so they can speak effectively to specific groups. Will they be expected to speak to specific types of collections, or strategies being used to connect with readers of this format? Do they read eBooks themselves and so have some direct experience of the devices, formats, and vendor options your library is using, or will you need to provide them with a hands-on overview?

You'll also want to talk with them about the short-term statistics you'll be tracking, the monthly usage statistics and budget changes as well as the longer-term trends you'll be monitoring. As talked about earlier in this chapter, both short-term changes and longer-term trends provide value, but they may tell you different things. Make sure you understand what types of data are most relevant to your stakeholders and be prepared to direct them to the better options for their needs.

It's also possible that your administration, board, and funders are looking to make connections between your eBook collection and other projects or initiatives that they are working on. If they are interested in developing strategies for using and supporting new technologies and digital literacy, help them make the connection to how eBooks are part of that broader community conversation. If they're working on issues related to schools and educational support or summer reading for children and teens, talk with them about what types of titles you're selecting for the collection that may align with what's needed to support students, or recreational reading for youth. If they're working on outreach to senior centers, or strengthening services for readers, make the connection between these initiatives and the opportunities provided by eBooks. These types of conversations may help strengthen support for your collection, and may also help provide you with some focus for where to get started, or where to grow.

CONCLUSION

As part of your overall planning for launching your eBook collection, you should include a plan for how you will measure it use, and the impact it will have on your overall collection and service. Starting with even a few benchmarks in circulation and access will help you understand how your collection is working for your patrons and will allow you to improve the way your patrons can use this collection and the services you have in place to support their use.

To take a comprehensive approach in evaluation, think through all of the places and ways that your eBook collection now interacts with your entire collection. Also look for how your eBook service interacts with your overall library service, from Reader's Advisory at a service point to book club support to in-library displays and promotion. Also, find the parts that are specific to your eBook service, from developing a new library program on how to download an eBook onto a device to developing a process to review the information from your vendors about how your eBook collection is being used. Think about what data makes sense to look at in the short term and what data makes sense to track in the longer term so you can see a truer picture of what is happening. Collecting data and thinking through what it means is time consuming, sometimes contradictory, and sometimes overwhelming. But using the data to make decisions will improve your service and will help you craft messages for your stakeholders.

Our library is evaluating our eBook collection and services. We'd like to hear from you about your interest in eBooks.

Did you know that our library offers eBooks?
- Yes
- No
- Uncertain

If yes, how often do you check out an eBook from the library's collection?
- More than two per month
- Less than two per month

Are you reading eBooks primarily for:
- School/homework
- Recreation or leisure
- Work topics
- Research

What types of eBooks do you check out? (Circle all that apply)
- Fiction
- Nonfiction

If you don't check out eBooks from the library, is it because: (Circle all that apply)
- You didn't know we offered eBooks
- You are not finding the titles you were looking for
- You found title that you were interested in, but the copies were checked out
- Other (please describe) ____

Anything else you'd like to tell us about our eBook collection?

____

____

What is your age range? (optional)
- 12–14
- 15–17
- 18–25
- 26–35
- 36–55
- 56–65
- 66–75
- 76–85
- 86+

Thank you for taking a few moments to give us your feedback. We appreciate it!

Figure 6.1   Sample Patron Survey

Our library is evaluating our eBook collection and services. We'd like to hear from you about your interest in eBooks.

One of the areas where we are considering adding eBooks is our fiction collection. Would you be interested in checking out eBooks in any of the following categories? (Circle all that apply)

Best sellers	Children's Fiction	Christian Fiction
Classics	Erotica	Fantasy
Historical Fiction	Literary Fiction	Mystery
Picture Books	Romance	Science Fiction
Teen Fiction	Thriller	Urban Fiction
Western		

Is there anything else you'd like to tell us about our eBook collection?

____

____

What is your age range? (optional)
- 12–14
- 15–17
- 18–25
- 26–35
- 36–55
- 56–65
- 66–75
- 76–85
- 86+

Thank you for taking a few moments to give us your feedback. We appreciate it!

Figure 6.2 Sample Patron Survey: Interest in Fiction

Our library is evaluating our eBook collection and services. We'd like to hear from you about your interest in eBooks.

One of the areas where we are considering adding eBooks is our nonfiction collection. Would you be interested in checking out eBooks in any of the following categories? (Circle all that apply)

Biography and Memoir	Business	Careers
Computers	Cookbooks	Crafts
Current Events	Do It Yourself	Finance
Fitness	Health and Medical	History
Humor	Math	Pets

Figure 6.3 Sample Patron Survey: Interest in Nonfiction

Philosophy   Photography   Politics

Psychology   Religion and Spirituality   Science

Self-Help   Technology   Test Guides

Travel

Other (please describe):

Is there anything else you'd like to tell us about our eBook collection?

____

____

What is your age range? (optional)

- 12–14
- 15–17
- 18–25
- 26–35
- 36–55
- 56–65
- 66–75
- 76–85
- 86+

Thank you for taking a few moments to give us your feedback. We appreciate it!

Figure 6.3   (Continued)

CHAPTER 7

Increasing and Expanding Your eBook Collection

While launching your new collection and services can be exciting, the best times for you and your patrons come once the eBooks are being checked out in enthusiastic numbers. Now that you've moved past the launch of your collection, you'd like to expand what you can offer your patrons, expanding the depth and breadth of what's available for them to use. Even if you'll need to proceed somewhat slowly, you'll still want to take the time to evaluate what you've learned from your launch to help your staff begin the next phase of this collection.

START WITH A PLAN

Hopefully, as you started with the work to launch your collection, you laid out your plan and your goals, at least for the first few months. If you didn't, it's never too late to take that step. It will be worth your time to take a step back and make sure you've covered all the bases for your launch, and to make sure you have the information you need to determine if you're ready to move ahead.

Whether you started with a plan you now need to update or are developing your first plan post-launch, when you started your eBook collection, you set at least a few things in place to get things under way. You allocated funding, selected materials, worked with your technical staff and vendors on platforms and other access areas, trained staff, and announced the new collection to your patrons. Even if you only did these steps at a very high level, you now should have at least a baseline of information about what you've done to date to use for the next phase of your work.

USING DATA TO DETERMINE WHAT TO PURCHASE

As mentioned in Chapter 6, you will want to determine what circulation data points you wish to use to evaluate the way patrons are using your collection. Now that you have some actual use data, you can better understand the strengths and weaknesses of the data points you have access to. If you are collecting data from both your integrated library system (ILS) and your vendor, you'll be able to see more clearly if they are counting the same things, or if there are some differences that you'll need to account for as you start reviewing the information to make your next round of collection purchases.

Once you have a better understanding of how your circulation data is working, you'll be ready to determine how you are going to use it in terms of creating a longer-term purchasing plan that will move you from start-up through the first year or so of your service. Perhaps you find that your patrons are avidly reading fiction, but are checking out relatively few nonfiction titles. Will you change your spending plan and weigh it in the favor of fiction? Or are there other service factors that need to be weighed in as well? Or perhaps you find that your eBook travel guides are always checked out and the circulation on the physical copies of travel guides is slowing down. Will you act on the data and purchase more eBook copies of travel books and fewer physical ones? Now that you're making a longer-term collection plan, you'll be able to lay out your priorities in this area, and develop some monthly or quarterly check-ins to evaluate what may be changing in these areas so your staff can know where to focus their purchasing.

ADDITIONAL COLLECTION DEVELOPMENT PLANNING

If you want to move to more of a certain type of material in your collection, do you want to focus on new titles being released or do you want to delve into your vendor's offerings to find backlist titles? Will focusing on newer titles or backlist be priorities for your entire collection, or will you want to make different decisions about depending on the specific part of the collection you're working on? As an example, perhaps you wish to expand what you offer in terms of mystery fiction for adults, and you've identified the overall budget you have available to allocate to expand this part of the collection. Based on the feedback you have from your patrons, and what you can see from your use data, you want to focus both on new fiction titles and on backlist titles. How are you going to find the titles and how are going to strike that balance between new and backlist titles?

There are numerous methods you can use as selection strategies as you start expanding your eBook collection. Obviously you need to choose ones that work in the time and resources you have available. As you discovered when developing your launch collection, one of the resources at your disposal is your vendors and their pre-selected lists. You also have data from your physical collection as well as any data you can collect directly from your patrons: suggestions for purchase, comment cards, focus groups, surveys, and so on. Those resources can help provide direction, and may even provide specific title or author suggestions to aid with this process.

If you are using a vendor or multiple vendors, one of the first strategies to employ would be to see how they might be able to help you, especially if you want develop a longer-term strategy to be used any time you wish to expand your collection. Staying with our mystery example, look or ask for lists from your vendor of the top-circulating mysteries in your area or in the country to get you started with your expanded selection. Perhaps you are able to provide the vendor with a list of your top-circulating mystery authors and ask that their collection development staff send back to you a cart of titles you don't have in your collection. Depending on the vendor tools, this type of search may be an easy one your selection staff can use to find titles. Each part of the collection you expand will have its own unique features, and in the case of our mystery example, popular titles often come in series. Do you want the whole series in eBook version? If that's an important criterion, you should ask your vendor or search your vendor's database for how many titles in the series they can provide. How will you handle a series where only a few of the titles are available as eBooks? Or if an author has changed publisher over the course of his or her career, all of the author's titles may be available through the vendor, but the titles may be sold with varying purchasing models. For instance, it's possible that the first 10 titles in the series are available under a model where a library can purchase a title once and have perpetual access. But starting with number 11 in the series, the author changed publishers and 11–20 are sold under the model where a title needs to be re-purchased every year. These are the types of questions and situations that may have been easy to skip over when you were setting up a basic collection, but they will need to be addressed, or at least acknowledged, as you expand your service and grow into the next phase of your collection.

Many eBook vendors employ librarians as part of their collection development staff, and these staff members support the creation of their title suggestion lists. Knowing that this type of expertise may be available, you may be able to ask your vendor to send carts of suggestions for titles and authors that your staff can use to increase your capacity and make your selection process more efficient. Building a relationship with your vendor, and aligning your selection process with what you have in place with other formats, will help integrate your eBook process into your broader workflow. This will be essential as you expand and stabilize your collection development with eBooks.

Vendors are also improving their selection and acquisitions tools for library staff. Obviously, vendors want to make it easy for you to buy eBooks from them. While the vendor's staff will be available to assist you, you can also easily run searches yourself. Depending on the collection area and vendor tool you may be able to narrow down quickly to a usable list of potential titles to review as possible purchases. Because vendors are often loading data into their system directly from the publishers, you will mostly likely find some titles in your search results that you would call false hits. In the case of our mystery example, you might find titles you would consider adult but the publisher has coded as teen. Comparing information coming from your library's system to what is coming from a vendor's system will always be problematic, since the original data sources are different. How much of a problem this will be for you and your staff will probably depend on the collection you are working with, and how familiar they are with the vendor tools and your collection. Gaining skills and familiarity will come as staff use the tools more frequently, but understanding the challenges in this area will help your staff as they start to expand your collection.

ADDING A NEW COLLECTION AREA

When you determine that you'd like to add a new collection area, based on what you're seeing in your circulation data and in patron feedback, the methods you've used already starting and expanding an existing collection will work here as well. Since you may not be as familiar with this new area, or at least with what's available in eBooks in this area, again you'll want to start with the techniques that are being described throughout this book. With a new collection area, look to any lists your vendors have available to help you, whatever information you have about your physical collection, feedback from your patrons, and what you might be learning about this collection area from reading about publishing trends.

The new collection area that you are contemplating could be an area where your patrons are suddenly expressing an interest in eBooks where they haven't before, or a new publishing trend where you don't have any experience or comparable print collections to use as a baseline to determine collection scope or patron interest. An example of this type of trend might be patron requests for titles that have never appeared in a physical edition. Some fiction authors are producing novellas as well as full-length novels as eOrginals, meaning that a book is first published in eBook format or published only in eBook format. An eOriginal is usually defined as an original story that has never appeared before. You may be getting requests for these titles directly from patrons through your "suggest a purchase" process or even through interlibrary loan requests, since your patrons may not know that the book is not available in a physical print version. And once again, you can use the same methodology as mentioned earlier; you can search your vendor's database for the individual titles that patrons have shared with you through your title suggestion process, or you can ask for lists of eOriginals to consider from your vendor.

Whatever collection you are thinking of expanding or adding, you'll want to be aware of options so that this new collection will be a good fit for your eBook readers. While the example of adding eOriginals is not too much of a stretch in terms of adding a collection area, eOriginals will generally align with titles and genres already in your library collection. Some areas your patrons are requesting may need to be reviewed more thoroughly since they may be pushing the edges of your collection scope. This is another place where it will be good to watch out for any of the budgetary impacts that may come from purchasing a more unknown type of collection area, especially with some of the purchasing models that may come with some of these types of materials.

If a new collection area is one that you would like to try out on a trial basis, this is a place where it's possible to use the limited use eBook licensing to your advantage. Perhaps you would like to see how some of the newer business titles appeal to your patrons. You can weight your purchases in favor of those that expire so that you will not have titles "sitting" in your collection if you find that your patrons don't end up checking them out, and instead prefer health and wellness titles. Of course, the downside to this type of trial is that you are tied to particular publishers and their purchasing models. You will be choosing a selection of titles from a limited group of titles rather than the entire pool of titles available. If you use this type of purchasing to try out a collection and it quickly proves successful, you may need to move out of the trial basis quickly. For example, you start a small history collection on a trial basis, and you focus your purchasing on titles from publishers with a limited number of loans model. You will need to know what you will do if your patrons ask you for popular history titles on current best-seller lists and you haven't included those titles in the collection because they are from publishers with longer-term models. If you receive repeated requests from patrons for other titles, you may need to expand your offerings quickly. While using purchasing models as a way to expand collections will not work in the long term, there are opportunities inherent in the purchasing models to be creative with how you can try out, fund, and support newer areas of interest.

SETTING GOALS AND LIMITS

A number of ways to approach budgeting for your eBook collection have been presented throughout this book. As you further develop your collection, you'll want to develop a deeper understanding of the publisher and vendor purchasing models so you can be prepared for the type of impact they'll have on the longer-term viability of your eBook collection. Budgeting for eBooks includes not only new purchases, but also repurchases of expiring content and additional copies to respond to demand, as well as any related costs like purchasing MARC records to add to your catalog. It's a complex system, and one that becomes more important to stay ahead of as your collection and service matures.

As you continue to plan for launching or expanding your collection, you'll want to determine if you need to establish any goals for overall circulation numbers for this collection, or if you need to set up any limits to purchasing. You may have fairly unlimited resources, or you may need to manage these parts of your collection and use closely. You'll develop a clearer vision of what's needed as you start getting actual use data from your patrons, but you'll also want to be clear with your staff if there are any limitations on collection growth, or any circulation targets that need to be met before the next phase of collection expansion can begin.

One area to consider is the threshold where you'll want to consider adding additional copies of a title based on patron demand. You may already have a "request to copy" ratio for your physical collection, and could consider just expanding that to your eBook collection to get started, or you may want to consider a new model based on what you see happening based on the use of your eBook collection. For every 10 requests, do you want to have 1 "copy" or a ratio of 10:1 of an eBook? Or is it 15:1, 7:1, 5:1, 3:1, or some other ratio? Since your collection is now being used, you'll have some data about how your patrons are using your collection and you may have a clearer idea of your goals for the collection. This will help you determine what you would like to accomplish in terms of responsiveness to patron activity, and what your budget and service will be able to support. You'll also be able to consider how your decision here relates to your "request to hold" ratio decisions for other formats, including physical books and audio books. It may take a while to set a limit that works well, especially since patron use right after you launch your collection might skew some of the activity you'll see once your collection has normalized and your patrons are more familiar with the service. A new service just like opening a new building often generates interest, but what are the use levels at six months or a year? At a minimum, you'll want to be prepared at least with what ratio you support at the beginning of your eBook launch, knowing you can continue to adjust this ratio as needed as your use and collection expands.

As you establish a framework for expanding your collection, you'll want to develop guidelines for how to review extending access to titles that are expiring in your collection. Will you plan to repurchase everything regardless of use, or will you expect to see a specific number of circulations per title before you continue to have it in the collection? For titles where your access is limited by the number of circulations, how quickly do you expect to see those used before you'd purchase additional access? It may take a while for you and your staff to determine what types of use you're seeing to come to any firm conclusions, but these are the types of things you'll want to start considering early in the process to help you be prepared to grow.

COLLECTION FORMATS SUPPORTED

Throughout this book discussion has been about tying the decisions you make regarding starting or expanding an eBook service to what is happening with your other collections, your other services, your other marketing efforts, and other places where your eBook collection overlaps with the other services your library provides. As your eBook collection moves from a beginning collection to a fully integrated part of your overall collection, it's good to think about how exactly and where eBooks fit into all of the formats you collect. At the moment it feels as if this is a time where new formats continue to expand, but no formats are truly becoming obsolete. It's also easy to simply add another new format without stepping back and seeing how that format fits into the whole of your library's collection. With the implementation of an eBook collection, you could now easily have in your collection a physical book version (with hardcover, trade paperback, and mass market versions), a large print edition, a book on CD version, an eAudio version and more, all of the same title. All of these versions are actively being produced by publishers. None of these formats is a "legacy" format. And now you have added an eBook version to the mix, and possibly more than one platform to purchase it as if you're working with multiple vendors. An audio version can be argued to be a somewhat different type of the book because of the role the narrator can play in interpreting the work, but you still might have two or three different "packages" of an audio version.

As you think about expanding your eBook collection, how does this new collection fit into any discussion you have about redundancy of formats? Do you have any stakeholders asking you how many versions of the same title you are purchasing because they're concerned about limiting your ability to purchase a deeper collection if you need to purchase so many versions of the same title? If you have secured additional or external funding to launch your eBook collection, this question may not be very meaningful as you're getting started. But should your funding priorities shift in order to implement the next format or service, it's important to know your priorities around how many formats you are willing to support, which are the most important, and what type of funding it will take to make it possible to purchase to meet those priorities. Knowing your goals will help if you are questioned about how many different times the library is purchasing the same title. The number of formats supported should also be part of your collection evaluation plan, since that will help you balance this new format within the complete context of your collection and service.

To help your library get started with this process, a sample collection planning checklist is provided at the end of this chapter (Figure 7.1).

DEVELOPING AN EVALUATION PLAN: HOW WILL DATA ABOUT PATRON USE OF THE COLLECTION SUPPORT YOUR GROWTH?

As you move ahead with planning and implementing your collection, you will want to develop and document a complete evaluation plan. That will help you stay on track with your goals, and stay within any limits you may have set as well. This is also a plan that could be shared with stakeholders so they're aware of what you're tracking and how often you plan to be reviewing and reporting information about what's happening with your collection. Having even a basic evaluation plan will help you stay accountable to your team and your stakeholders, and will help you respond to changes in the broader environment also.

WHAT DATA WILL YOU COLLECT?

As discussed in earlier chapters, there are lots of potential types of data and related information you can collect about what's happening with your eBook collection. There are times where less can definitely be more. Simply collecting data especially if that data doesn't help you meet your goals or evaluate your service isn't helpful. You'll be better served by starting with a few key areas that are relevant to you and your stakeholders than by tracking every possible piece of information. You can add additional types of data as you continue to expand your service, but you don't need to start with all the possible options.

Obviously, there are many aspects of collection building to consider: expanding existing collections, adding new collections, setting circulation goals and limits, yet again determining how your eBook collection fits into the whole of your collection, and creating a collection evaluation plan. You'll also want to understand what your patrons are doing and what you can learn about their experience. And you'll want to look for areas where this collection aligns with other parts of your library service, to make sure you can clearly see the connections and any potential gaps in service.

DEVICES SUPPORTED

Now that patrons are actually using your collection, you'll be better able to see what types of devices they're using to read the books they're checking out. You may have had some estimates about what types of devices would be most popular based on your pre-launch survey of your patrons and other feedback from staff and vendors as you launched your collection. You'll now be able to check your pre-launch expectations here against actual use, and make adjustments in your collection, technical help, and other services that you can see that your patrons are actually using now that they're able to check out library eBooks.

The types of devices your patrons use to read eBooks is an area where you'll want to track both short-term trends, such as monitoring what devices your patrons are using right now to get their books, and longer term trends, such as watching to see if they are increasing their use of a new device, and decreasing use of another device. This is an area where you should expect to see change, mostly coming from factors beyond the library and outside your control. Tablets, smartphones, and dedicated eReaders are all commercial, consumer devices and new ones come into the market all the time. The devices get damaged and need to be replaced as well. You'll need to be able to adjust to these new devices, with potential new features, as part of your planning process. Of course, many of your patrons may also be working with older devices, even devices that are not supported by your vendors, which will also have an impact on the types of formats you purchase and the level of technical support you may need to provide.

This is definitely an area where what's happening outside the library will have an important impact on what your patrons are doing. While dedicated eReaders like the Nook, the Kobo, and earlier Kindles used to be the primary types of devices used for eBooks, users are moving away from those types of dedicated devices to more multipurpose devices like smartphones and tablets. This change may also impact the way patrons connect with your collection. Some devices may work better with the vendor apps, moving patrons away from your catalog or website, or from the vendor website. As you review how your patrons are reading today, watch for those shifts in the types of devices they're using so you can be prepared to support them going forward.

TRAINED STAFF

As you move from launching or expanding your collection to making it part of your regular business, you'll want to review any adjustments you need to make to your service strategy as well as to your collection plan. You based your first service plan on patron feedback about what they expected to do, and you now have experience with how they actually are, or aren't, using your collection. This is the perfect time to step back and review the way you're connecting with patrons about your eBooks and see if there are changes or adjustments that would strengthen your service plan.

One of the first places to start is to check in with your staff about what's happening with customer service now that they're working directly with patrons. If you'd started with developing basic expectations about what staff should know to assist patrons with eBook questions, you'll probably know right away if your staff really is prepared. Or if instead you need to revisit your training plan and spend more time helping staff get up to speed. This is also the time to really start working on your plan to make your staff training model sustainable. You'll have a better idea of what new devices you may need to purchase for staff training. You'll also know how much time your staff will need both to set aside keep their skills sharp and also to learn about new functionality coming from vendors and publishers.

Your staff members are one of the main ways your patrons will learn about your eBook collection, and they play an especially important role with patrons who are new to eBooks or who run into technical issues with their devices or vendor tools. They also play an important role in connecting your eBook users to your overall services for readers and making sure that your services include your eBook readers. Confident, competent staff is a key part of your ability to promote your eBook collection, and it's definitely important to make sure that you invest time on staff training.

If you decided to offer public programs or classes to help patrons become more comfortable with using your collection and their devices, this will be the time to review your attendance data. You'll want to see if these programs are reaching the people who need these services and if the programs you're offering are actually helping your patrons learn the skills they're looking for. At a minimum, you'll want to look at your overall attendance data. You'll be able to see the average number of patrons attending each session, as well as what locations, times of day, or other criteria are bringing in the most patrons.

Beyond that basic information, you'll want to confirm that once patrons attend one of your programs they have the resources they need to go home or into your library and check out eBooks from your collection. To better understand the impact your programs are having, you'll want to make sure you're asking patrons to evaluate their experience at your programs. You may also want to consider asking if you can follow up with them after the session to see if they have what they need to get eBooks onto their devices.

Attendance at public programs can vary widely by library. This is definitely a part of the service that you'll want to evaluate closely, since setting aside staff time to develop and implement an eBook program may not be the most cost-effective way for your library to support patrons who need in-person assistance with their eBooks and devices. Drop-in labs, making staff available for appointments, or sending staff out to community locations may work better in your community than traditional library-based programming. Evaluating what you're seeing in program data will be an important part of making sure you're allocating limited staff resources to the areas where they'll have the most impact.

In addition to reviewing your structured public programs, you'll want to take a look at your overall readers and information service and see if there are changes you want to make to improve the way you are able to support patrons who stop by your buildings or check in online about their eBooks. If you've been asking staff to track the number or type of eBook questions they're getting at your public service points, this is a good time to review what you're seeing there and adjust your strategy if needed. Are staff members getting most questions at the service desk, or when they're talking with patrons browsing the collection? Did adding a poster about your eBook collection at your service point increase patron questions, or did the number of questions from patrons stay the same? Taking a look at what's happening at your service points will help you better understand the types of questions patrons are asking, where they're asking them, and how best to get them the information they're looking for.

You have many ways to evaluate how your staff can help connect patrons with this collection and help make sure that patrons are aware of what's available and how to access it. This data from your service points should be reviewed alongside your data on public programming. You may find that your patrons prefer just to drop in or call the library when they need assistance and not to wait for a program to learn how to use their devices. Or you may see many patron questions in your online reference service, since patrons are already on your website looking at eBooks when they have questions, and prefer to get their questions answered through online channels. eBook patrons are often remote patrons, and may be using your services for remote patrons at a higher level than they're using your in-library services. Making sure you have your staff allocated at the right service points will make sure your patrons get the help they need, and will help make your service more effective.

INTEGRATION INTO A BROADER SERVICE STRATEGY

As you start learning more about how patrons will be using your collection, you'll want to take the opportunity to review how you are integrating your eBooks into your overall service for your patrons. When you started your planning process, you postulated who you expected to use your collection: possibly adult fiction readers, possibly students for homework, possibly cookbook and memoir readers, and you designed some of your preliminary outreach strategies to connect with them. Now that you're starting to see who your first users are, you should take a step back and evaluate if you're on track to reach them, and how you are making connections for them to and from your other services.

It's easy to think of eBook readers as a unique group of users, and in some ways they are. They have some unique needs, mostly related to the format itself, and connecting with them around those issues is important. But in many ways, they have the same needs as any library user, and in fact, they probably use many other parts of your service as well. As you move from letting everyone know you have a new collection to managing an ongoing service, you'll want to move from treating eBooks as something new and unique to something that's connecting across all of your collections. It can take a while to get used to including eBooks in your in-library and online displays, or to ask patrons if they're looking for a print or eBook copy of a book, but the more the staff can make those connections, the more you'll reach new users in a more organic way. But you may need to be intentional to start with; it may help for staff to share ideas about how they talk with patrons successfully about eBooks during regular reference or readers advisory conversations to start to build confidence and learn some new habits. Despite all of your marketing campaigns and posters, making sure your staff is able to make the connection and hand-sell the service will still be a primary way some of your patrons learn about your collection and decide to give it a try.

MARKETING STRATEGY

Each library approaches marketing and promotion in its own way. The opportunities to promote library services can vary widely in each community. Your library may have a column in the local or neighborhood newspaper or a regular time on a local radio or TV station. You may be lucky enough to have your own promotion staff, or you may have someone who does this type of work on the fly. However you approach marketing and promotion, you'll want to make sure you spend some time reviewing your options and determine which one is the best fit for the parts of your community you're trying to reach.

This is especially true as you move past launch to a more ongoing, sustainable model for promoting this collection. Announcing a new collection or service can be relatively easy, and you may even have had dedicated funding available to support getting the word out. You're more likely to get print and broadcast media time for something new than for something you've been doing for several months or longer. Now that you're managing an ongoing service, you'll need to look for new ways to let people know about what you have to offer them in terms of eBooks.

Two main areas are to be considered when planning in this area: in-library promotion and external promotion.

In-library promotion is, of course, most likely to reach your regular patrons, or people who already use the library. They may come in daily, monthly, or only a few times a year. But they are probably at least generally aware of what your library has to offer, but might not have had an eReader or other device when they last visited the library. They will benefit from your plan to meet them where they are: using the library services that are of interest to them, and potentially being interested in eBooks at some point in the future if the collection lines up with their needs.

You'll want to use your basic understanding about how these patrons use your services to figure out how to reach them when they visit the library. If they browse your fiction shelves and don't see the book they're looking for, how would they know that you might have an eBook available? If they're working on a homework assignment and all of the books on their topic are checked out, how will they think to check your online collection? Think about ways to connect with patrons where they are in your building, especially if they're looking for books in areas where you're purchasing eBooks. Many patrons who stop by your library may never talk with staff, so you'll want to make sure your plan to reach these regular users includes ways to connect with these self-reliant regular users of your service so they'll know this new collection is available for them, even though they can't see the books on the shelves.

To reach in-library patrons, you may want to consider posters, bookmarks, business cards, or similar give-ways that they can pick up and take with them. These are a standard way that libraries promote their services, and it's easy to expand this model to promote your eBook collection. You may have had some of these developed for your launch, so it would be easy to update them with a new message as your collection expands and your service matures. These resources are also easy to repurpose for library staff visits to community locations, making these print promotional materials more flexible than some of the other options that you could use.

Standalone and in-shelf book displays are an important way that libraries support browsing and discovery, helping patrons discover titles and topics that they might not have found on their own. But how do you do a display of eBooks? This is another place where in-library promotional posters and similar materials are needed to connect patrons with your eBook collection. Signage can be basic, letting users know that there are more books available online, or could be more focused, letting them know which types of materials or specific authors they'll find in your eBook collection. Ideally, your staff could develop both options and see which is more effective with patrons, so they're able to develop a message that makes the best connection between the physical and eBook collection choices available to your patrons.

External promotion is an equally important area to consider as you move into messaging about your ongoing service. In many cases, the best promotion you have is your library website and social media channels. While these are great ways to reach potential users, they may also primarily be reaching the same patrons you're reaching with your in-library promotions: patrons who already use the library and are familiar with your services. However, these channels allow you to reach patrons at home and at the office, where they may find eBooks to be a more appealing opportunity, since checking out your collection online might save them a trip to the library building. Your ability to manage your website and social media directly will depend on your local practice, so there may be some limitations on what you can do in this area. But channels like social media can be powerful ways to connect with users and they will also give you some good data to use as you evaluate which ways to connect with patrons are most effective.

If you have booklists or similar resources on your website, consider how you will integrate your eBooks into these resources. Will you add separate lists for eBooks? Will your general mystery or biography lists include eBooks as well, and if so, how will people know that there are both print and eBook copies available? As you grow into your collection and get more comfortable with what your patrons are looking for, you'll get a better feel for what will work. Library booklists help direct patrons to specific titles or topics; you will get the added benefit of being able to track how successful these are as a way to connect readers to eBooks. You may be able to track the impact of the booklists by watching the number of reserves and circulations on the titles on the list.

You'll also want to review what messages you're sharing on social media. Social media is a good way to reach your patrons, and is also increasingly a way that print and broadcast media is gathering information about what's happening in the community. You'll want to make sure you have a strategy for ongoing messaging here, since it's a fun and flexible way to make connections, and also get patron feedback. Most social media channels provide use data also, making this an easy way to track how effective your outreach is in this area.

While many of your eBooks users may use other parts of the library also, when they're looking for eBooks, they're probably not physically in your library building. There are also patrons who only use the library remotely, so they'll never see your in-library displays or promotions. You'll want to make sure that you consider them, and the ways they learn about library services, as you build out a more sustainable promotion strategy post-launch.

Your library may already have a process in place to review the impact your marketing and promotions have had on the use of your eBook collection. If you regularly track the amount of business that comes your way after an article in the local paper or a post on your website, you'll want to make sure you're doing that for the promotion of your eBook collection. You'll find methods that are more effective for your community, either to increase use by current users or to reach new users, and those are the areas you'll want to focus on as you work to expand the use of your collection.

IS THERE A LIMIT TO WHAT YOU CAN SUPPORT?

We usually consider growth and increased use as a good thing, and in most cases, it is. You're reaching more people, you've selected the books they really want, your online access works smoothly. What's not to love?

In most cases, these signs are a good indicator that things are going well for your library and your patrons. But growth can sometimes lead to pressures on your staff, services, collections, and budgets that are beyond what you can support. One example of this was mentioned in the discussion of number of formats purchased of the same title, where adding eBooks means that instead of purchasing a new title, you may instead be purchasing yet another copy of a title that you already own, but in a new format. Supporting an increasingly popular eBook collection could mean that the overall diversity of your collection gets smaller, since you're primarily purchasing additional copies of titles that are already available to your patrons. This may be an unexpected outcome of a successful eBook collection.

Your staff and patrons are probably familiar with waiting lists on print materials. Staff know how to help patrons manage them, how to talk with patrons about them, and how they work to support overall access to your library's collection. As mentioned in the section on collection goals and limits, you will need to determine how to use waiting list data to decide when to purchase more copies of popular titles. You may not always know what titles are going to get long lists, but you may already have a process in place for your print, and probably a funding model as well, so your selection staff has a framework for responding to patron needs when these lists meet a specified limit.

As you launch your eBook collection, the same thing will probably need to happen there. Your patrons learn that you have eBooks, and they will start reserving the eBooks as they do with your print collection. The length of the lists will depend on the local policies you set around how many titles a patron can have checked out and how many reserves he or she can have waiting for them. You should still expect to see waiting lists on popular titles, or on parts of the collection where you may only have a small number of titles for patrons to choose from. This may be true when your collection is small and there aren't a lot of titles available. It may also be true as your collection grows, especially if use of your eBook collections matches how your patrons are using your physical collection within certain genres or subjects. Being prepared to respond to needs here, ideally in the same way as you respond to similar pressures placed on your physical collection, will be an important part of meeting patron expectations and making sure your collection growth is sustainable.

Your patrons may also not understand why they have to wait for an eBook the way they have to wait for a print book. You may get questions from them about the length of your waiting lists, since their expectation for this part of your collection may not be the same as they have for other parts of your collection. Some of this is part of helping your users understand how your eBook collection is designed to work and how you have access to the titles, and some of this is just managing user expectations, especially when they are excited to use this new service. Making sure library staff are able to help patrons with these kinds of questions will help ensure that patrons have a good understanding of what's possible in the short term, and what might be possible in the longer term as your collection matures.

While growing circulation is the sign of a healthy collection, it clearly also comes with some challenges. This will be especially true if you are starting with a small budget, since you'll have limited resources to work with to meet potentially high patron expectations. Do you use those limited funds to buy more copies to bring down the waiting lists, or do you use your budget for new titles to expand your overall collection? There's no right answer to this question, but you'll want to have thought through your options early in the process so you're prepared for this situation. You'll then know how to talk about your choices with stakeholders, staff, and patrons.

The other area where your success may have some unintended consequences is with your staff. As the use of your collection starts to grow, you may start seeing more and more patrons contacting you with eBook questions. They may be basic and fairly straightforward questions, or they may be technically complicated. You may start offering programs on using eBooks, or setting up drop-in labs for patrons to come in with questions. While your service responses will depend on the communities you serve, there will be patron questions, service needs, and programs that you and your staff didn't have before you launched your collection. While all these bring great new opportunities to connect with your patrons, integrating these new needs into your existing services may be a challenge. If you add eBook programs, is there something else you're not able to do? If your staff members are learning about all of the new devices they need to support, is there other training they're not able to attend? You have decided that adding eBooks to your collection is the right choice, but you'll want to be prepared to adjust your staff priorities to align the changes in your broader service that they may bring. Just as adding eBooks doesn't necessarily mean you'll see a decline in the use of other parts of your collection, adding eBook programs doesn't mean your patrons will want fewer storytimes or visits to the local senior center. It's an expansion of service with potential impacts on your staff's ability to support or expand services in other areas also.

HOW WILL YOU ADDRESS ANY GAPS IN THE DATA YOU ARE COLLECTING?

As you begin to evaluate the impact adding eBooks is having on your library, you may find that there are things you'd like to know more about that you're not able to track. These could be areas where you currently collect information about your physical collection or other parts of your services that aren't available for your eBook collection. This could be because they're not something the vendor can provide for you, or because they don't work as well for eBooks as they do for other types of materials. Or, if your patron use is low, the data you collect may not be deep enough to be useful or for changes to be statistically significant.

Whatever the reason, you'll want to make sure you can account for any data gaps you may encounter and be able to speak to what they mean for your ability to evaluate your eBook collection. If your stakeholders are used to seeing a specific type of data and you're not able to provide it here, you'll want to be able to explain that and see if there are other ways to address what's missing. If it's too early to use some of the data you have because the totals are still small, you'll want to be able to estimate when you expect use to be at a level when you can start including it in your evaluation plan. It is expected that you may have gaps in the data you'd like to collect. But being prepared to work through where you have gaps and where you have a full spectrum of data will help make sure you are fully utilizing all of the information you have available to you.

Data may also be leading you in a certain direction to make certain decisions. If the data doesn't "feel" right, you need to delve into the data and also into what is behind your "feeling." Sometimes you don't have the right data, sometimes you don't have all the data, and sometimes you are surprised with the conclusions the data is leading you to, and you need to take the time to process the data. If it turns out you are missing a piece of data, see if it's available to add into your decision-making process. If there is data you need from a vendor and you don't see it in the reports, follow up with them to see if it's available. It may be within a report that you weren't aware of or they may be able to provide it to you.

Gaps in the data are to be expected. As you make your next round of decisions and plans, you'll want to note the shortcomings. You do want your decisions to be based on the data points you have selected and based on data points you feel confident in.

CREATING A COLLECTION MAINTENANCE PLAN

Because eBook collections are still relatively new in public libraries, the role of weeding an eBook collection is a new topic as well. Libraries are busy expanding their collections and reaching new users, and may be focused less on ways to scale back and remove titles that they've purchased. It may feel too soon to consider how to determine how best to manage collections that aren't taking up physical "space" and with covers and pages that are never showing wear. Does it matter that an eBook hasn't circulated for several years if it's not taking up limited physical space that is needed for newer titles on the shelves of your library building? eBooks are becoming a more familiar format in the public consciousness and in our libraries. As eBooks become a standard collection format, then maintaining the collection becomes part of your professional responsibility, and one that needs your attention.

IS IT TIME FOR MUSTIE FOR eBOOKS?

Yes. If you are planning to have a successful eBook collection, then that plan needs to include a way to maintain the collection. Creating a maintenance plan and finding the time to implement that plan has a different set of challenges than weeding a physical collection.

For one thing, as just mentioned, an eBook collection is easier to ignore. It's not taking up space in the same way physical books do, and if you work in a library building you're probably not reminded of pressing weeding issues the same way you are when you pass shelves of books every day.

MUSTIE is a quick method that has been used to start a weeding discussion and decision. MUSTIE can be used as a start in evaluating collections. Obviously, it was designed for physical collections, but it can be adapted and used for eBooks as well. MUSTIE is usually defined as follows:

M   Misleading or factually inaccurate
U   Ugly (worn beyond repair)
S   Superseded
T   Trivial
I   Irrelevant
E   Elsewhere

Misleading or factually inaccurate: If you're weeding eBooks for the first time, this is great place to start. Great targets to start with are the books in which the content updates itself regularly. If you have a regular process for weeding your physical collection for areas that date quickly such as travel, legal resources, medical issues, or test guides, you'll want to expand those guidelines to your eBook collection. The same criteria should apply to all formats.

Ugly (worn beyond repair): The one letter that doesn't generally apply to eBooks, since the books don't experience the same wear and tear as physical books do. One area to consider could be cover art; as your collection ages, you may start to notice that the cover art is increasingly dated. If this is an issue for your patrons, you'll want to consider reviewing your collection with this criterion.

Superseded: Travel guides are always a great example of titles that supersede themselves. New editions are published each year with the most recent information, making the older copies less relevant. If you already have guidelines for these types of materials for your print collection, you'll want to use them for your eBooks as well.

Trivial: Is the biography of the top pop star from three years ago still circulating? If so, it's not trivial. If yes, it has stopped circulating, the title may indeed be trivial or less relevant, and it should be considered for weeding.

Irrelevant: Do you have anything in eBook form that it doesn't make sense to have any longer? Libraries purchased many books on Y2K, but soon after the turn of the century, those books were quickly irrelevant. Another example might be books published in an election year. After the election, many of these titles quickly become irrelevant, especially if they featured candidates who didn't win. In most cases, moving these types of eBooks out of your collection should be a priority.

Elsewhere: In the land of physical items, elsewhere refers to "Is there another place you can get the item from easily if your patrons want it: through a library near yours, through interlibrary loan, etc.?" Elsewhere in the world of eBooks is beginning to change as library consortia are evolving and becoming involved with offering eBooks. But an elsewhere to also be aware of is eBooks that you have in your collection that your patrons are obtaining elsewhere. One example might be information on learning a language. Perhaps you have information not only in physical formats (books and audio book in CD) but also eAudios, eBooks, and in databases. You may find that your patrons are not using your eBook offerings, but rather prefer what you are offering "elsewhere," even within your own collection. In this example of language learning, the content will not date quickly, and you may not feel the need to weed out titles if they're not expiring. But there may be some subject areas where you discover your patrons prefer materials they are obtaining elsewhere and you do want to remove eBook content.

If and when you do decide to weed eBook content, take time to create a weeding process. Just as when we weed physical items from our collections, there are multiple steps to think about when removing eBooks. With physical books you need to remove not only the item from the shelf but also the item information from your ILS system. Your eBook information may live in several places, for instance, both in your catalog and in your website. Investigate where all of the references to an eBook "live" and as you weed make sure you are deleting all instances. You also may have to investigate who has the technical permissions to remove data.

As you get more time and experience with eBooks and your eBook collections, best practices for maintaining the relevance of collections are certain to be developed. But if you are now beyond your trial period with your eBook collection and don't know how to start with the possibility of weeding, creating a MUSTIE with your own definitions is a way to start.

CONCLUSION

As you make the leap from your opening eBook collection into expansion and stability, we believe it's worth taking the time to take a step back to look at what you've done to get started and incorporate your lessons learned into the next phases of your plan for your eBook collection and service. Use the data you've collected to determine where and how to expand your eBook collection permanently and which collections to explore on a trial basis. Review the staff training and public programs you've offered to patrons. Just as businesses sometimes get into trouble by expanding too fast, do you need to look at any limits to your growth with regards to eBooks, both in terms of your collection and in terms of marketing or programming?

As you are moving out of your launch phase and into having eBooks as a part of your ongoing collection and service, it's time to look at how you are going to maintain both the collection and service. Maintaining your eBook collection means wrestling with how eBooks fit into all the formats you collect and what priority eBooks have in terms of collecting and funding. Maintenance also means looking at your collection regularly to see if there are titles that need to be removed. Maintaining your service is looking at what you have learned from patrons and staff as you have started with eBooks and incorporating that knowledge into the next iterations of your service.

With your new eBook collection, you will have whole new set of data points at your disposal. Looking at the data critically, knowing the strengths and weaknesses of the data and knowing where you may have gaps will strengthen your decision making when moving forward. Having an in-depth knowledge about your data points, the good and the bad, will also benefit you when reporting on your current service and future service to your stakeholders.

This document is designed to track how your eBook collection fits into your library's plan for your entire collection. It can be used to help track the maximum number of copies you want to purchase for the collection, the request to copy ratio used to purchase additional copies with significant patron demand, and funding allocations across the collection. It can be adapted to the specific needs and formats used by your library.

Quantity considerations: Is there a maximum number of copies to be purchased for the collection?
   Maximum number of copies to be purchased in regular print (hardcover, trade paperback, mass market paperback) _______
   Maximum number of copies to be purchased in large print _______
   Maximum number of copies to be purchased in eBook _______
   Maximum number of copies to be purchased in audiobook on CD _______
   Maximum number of copies to be purchased in eAudio _______
   Maximum number of copies to be purchased in pre-loaded audio players _______

Funding for eBooks
   Percentage of total budget allocated for eBooks _______
   Percentage of budget allocated for new titles _______
   Percentage of budget allocated for repurchasing expiring content _______
   Percentage of budget allocated for request to copy purchases _______

Patron requests in comparison to number of copies available. What is the goal for a request to copy ratio in the following categories?
   Request to hold ratio regular print _______
   Request to hold ratio large print _______
   Request to hold ratio eBook _______
   Request to hold ratio audiobook on CD _______
   Request to hold ratio eAudio _______
   Request to hold ratio preloaded audio players _______

Repurchasing metered or expiring eBook content
   Number of circulations needed in order to prompt a repurchase
      Within the last 2 years _______
      Within the last 1 year _______
      Within the last 6 months _______
   Examples of other considerations
      Title still generating holds?
      Part of a series?
      Author recognition?
      Seasonal title?

Figure 7.1   Sample Collection Planning Document

CHAPTER 8

Other Considerations

As you consider offering eBooks or expanding your collection, hopefully what's been discussed throughout this book will guide you as you determine what options will be the best choices for your library. In this chapter, a few related topics that are good to keep in mind as you interact with the world of eBooks are presented.

You were given enough general information, questions, and suggestions to use as you make decisions without being too prescriptive about what you should do for your library. With the pace of change happening in this area, we wanted to avoid providing too many specific details that could easily become out of date or less relevant soon after writing, and instead lay out a framework for starting or expanding an eBook collection that could be used as changes continued in the broader environment. Our primary goal was to provide ways to set directions and create plans for launching an eBook collection with examples and options that could be adjusted to a library's specific situation. Frequent change within the world of eBooks should be expected, even though it may not always be welcomed.

With the expanding mix of devices, file types, applications, publishing rules, pricing models, methods of access, and variety of integrated library system (ILS) software choices, as discussed in Chapter 2, it is amazing that a library lending model for eBooks works at all. Parts of the system, including devices, file types, and applications, are "owned" or developed by different sectors of the marketplace and by different companies. Few of those companies building some of these components have libraries as their primary focus. This means that as companies develop products, they're not necessarily developed with libraries or library patrons as the primary audience. When that is the case, then library eBook systems have to adapt to what's happening in the broader environment. One of the best ways to manage and adapt to inevitable change is to keep an eye open for what may be heading our way.

Everyone can point to experiments in technology that didn't take off, like those first dedicated eReaders in the 1990s. But as mentioned several times, the first eReaders did herald the coming of the ones that did start to have an impact in the mid-2000s, and that next round of eReaders were in the right place at the right time. The new eReaders had the shape, the weight, the look, the price, and the functionality that appealed to a wide range of potential users, and were in the marketplace when similar changes were happening with other devices and other media. In a short amount of time, we had a thriving eBook marketplace and then had companies figuring out how to make this new opportunity work for libraries, as well as the broader consumer marketplace.

Knowing about ideas and trends in industries that interact with the library eBook world or the eBook world in general will help you when a vendor reaches out to you asking you to buy, implement, or subscribe to the product it is promoting to you. If you can put its product into the context of the wider world, you are probably making a better decision, and certainly a more informed decision. There may also be trends and products that you see that you can in turn ask your vendors about, or turn internally to your colleagues at your library to ask, "Do we want to do this? Could we do this?" In a world where the question "Are libraries still relevant?" is asked in mainstream media each time a technological shift happens in the marketplace, following trends allows libraries to shift and adapt rather than react. At the very least, knowing the shifts and trends happening both inside and outside the library world allows you to have an answer to respond again to the question "Is the library still relevant, now that we have _______?" And your answer can be: "Yes, because we have _______, and are doing _______."

THE PUBLISHING WORLD

One of the important areas to watch is related to what's happening in the publishing world. Libraries buy many books, but they don't buy as many as the general reading public as a whole. If you can, keep an eye on what the major U.S. publishers are thinking and doing. Look for information about what they're publishing in eBook format. Are they providing eBooks for everything in their current publishing season? Are there some types of materials that are available only in a physical format? Or are there any titles or types of materials that they are publishing only as an eBook? If you are noticing changes in what you're able to purchase in physical or eBook form, look for what you can find about what might be behind these types of changes. Just as a library may start an eBook collection by identifying a few target audiences, you should be able to notice trends within press releases, interviews, or other announcements from publishers, since these are the places where they will often clarify whom they are trying to reach with a new publishing track. While the publishers will probably not give the actual data they compiled to make their decision, they may hint at some of the data. The press release may refer to the publisher wishing to give readers more of a particular kind of fiction, for instance. From this you can speculate that the type of fiction they reference might be doing quite well for the publisher in eBook form and this is an effort to expand their offerings.

Likewise, tracking what's happening within the world of small presses is helpful too. It is impossible to track every small press, but if you have small presses in your service area or you know that your patrons are especially interested in the output of particular presses, it's good to keep track of their eBook trajectory. Are they publishing everything they put out in both print and eBook version? The differences in publishing paths often point to what is selling or not for the publisher. You can look at that information and see whether it matches up with what is circulating from your collections, both in print and in eBook.

Luckily, there are many standard venues that track the publishing world, following both the big publishing houses and the main small presses. There are publications like Publishers Weekly reporting on the constant changes within the industry, as well as many blogs that track publishing trends and a wide variety of social media streams devoted to the publishing industry. There are also publishing representatives who often make information available; most major houses now have reps who are devoted to staying connected to libraries and librarians. May be, many small presses, especially ones in your service area, are happy to talk about what's changing in their world. Changes in the publishing world may affect your eBook planning, and they may also have an impact on what's available for you to purchase in print also, so it's an area to watch.

Of course, what is a trend in the publishing world may not become a trend in the library world. While watching what's happing on the publishing front, you'll also want to continue to review what you are seeing from patron behavior and interactions at your own library and adjust accordingly. If there is the sudden explosion of a certain type of fiction and your patrons are requesting it as well, that scenario is pretty easy to adapt to. As long as the publishers of that type of fiction make it available for library purchase, you can add that fiction to your collection. If you're purchasing eBooks from publishers directly for your own platform, or if it's in your library vendor's catalog of titles, you can obtain what you need in the same methods as you have always done. You'll need to adjust your budget and selection plans to adapt to this new trend, but your library already has at least a basic process or plan in place to make these kinds of changes as they develop.

But if suddenly there are titles being written to be read on cell phones, or perhaps on newer devices like watches that provide Internet access, that may be a difficult trend to adapt to even if your patrons want it from the library. There are already books being published that are optimized for these smaller screens, with the understanding that these readers may be reading on-the-go. The stories are often short in length, serialized or released chapter-by-chapter, and written using texting shortcuts and emoticons. Right now this type of publishing serves a smaller niche market, but imagine that these stories become hugely popular with a wider audience, and now you're being asked by your patrons why you don't have the stories in your eBook collection yet, and when you're going to add them. There may be new technical issues with this development and ones that may take time for library technology to catch up to.

Likewise, there are currently dispensers in train stations that provide short stories to commuters at the press of a button; these may be just a passing fancy, or they may come to have a longer-term impact. The public may find the short stories utterly engaging and are filling a niche that they hadn't even known was empty. There could be authors whose talents fit perfectly the format of a machine, giving travelers a story that can be read in under five minutes. If this type of storytelling becomes wildly popular, perhaps libraries will be adding story dispensers in our lobbies or next to an eBook kiosk. And perhaps, libraries will need more dispensers and fewer eBooks as a result of the trend. Or perhaps short-story dispensers will fade from view in a few months.

Sometimes publishers look to libraries for inspiration. One publisher has started a reader's advisory phone line during holiday shopping time to help readers find the perfect book for a gift. Reader's advisory is a service that many librarians feel is core to our profession. Now there is a company that is performing one of our core services. Granted the publishers are limited to what only the titles they have published, while librarians have a much bigger universe to choose from to use as recommendations for patrons. But perhaps a publisher earns a reputation for excellent customer service and patrons love their recommendations; will that affect the service that librarians offer? What if a library eBook vendor offered an online chat service that would provide reader's advisory to patrons who are using your eBook website? Would that be something your library would consider offering?

Because of their digital nature, eBooks offer opportunities that don't exist in the physical book world. Besides exploring new delivery mechanisms for books and different ways to connect with consumers, publishers are experimenting with what readers respond in terms of embedding functionality into the text itself: maps, videos, pop-ups that provide more information about what's covered in the book, sound and audio files, dictionaries, and so on. What if one of the elements that is embedded into the text is a purchase that a patron can make? The reader could be reading a book where a character is listening to a favorite song, and there within the text is a link that connects to a vendor site where the reader can purchase the song itself. Within moments, readers could purchase the song and have it playing in the background as they continue reading. Functionality like this is usually developed for the commercial or retail market, which means that it is normally intended to be used in a one-device/one-user situation. If the person who purchased the eBook has a credit card linked to the device he or she is using, that will allow the person to easily go to another website and make a purchase. But now your library is asked by patrons to buy this book, with this embedded functionality that was designed for a one-user/one-device model. How would this work in the library world? Even in this example, there are multiple options: choosing to not buy the eBook, asking to buy copies with the technology disabled, or buying the eBook with the embedded functionality intact. Of course, there are issues with all three of these options. Choosing to not buy a book that your patrons want and that fits within your collection scope is problematic. Choosing to disable the functionality means that your library patrons would have a different reading experience from people who bought the book from an online bookstore. Choosing to buy the book with the embedded functionality may mean that your library would need to work with your patrons on any technical issues that may arise.

In most cases the answer is yes; you do want to provide the book, ideally with the added functionality, but there may be a delay between what shows up in the marketplace and when you can offer it to patrons. You have to wait as technical options for libraries are developed, for vendors to make them available for us, or for ways to address the issues that make library use more challenging. You may need to update your collection and service policies to make a place for these new options, since, in the case of this example, you may be technically able to work with this new type of book, but you may have policies or practice that precludes you from directing patrons to commercial sites. Keeping track of the thinking and experimentation happening in the publishing world allows you to prepare answers for your patrons who ask if you are getting the serialized cell phone novel or the book where you can not only do "x" but also buy access to "y." It helps you prepare your stakeholders way in advance of when you need them to support you with technical or policy adjustments to respond to patron demand.

While it's impossible to know all the ways these types of trends will play out, staying aware of what's happening in the broader publishing world is important, even if the impact of some of the changes hasn't made its way to the library market or your community yet. Just as libraries experiment with ideas, so do publishers and there are lots of new ideas being explored by publishers. Some of these ideas could be things you want to consider implementing locally, adapt for a library setting, or promote to your patrons to make their eBook experience more enjoyable.

eBOOKS IN THE LIBRARY SETTING

While it's important to watch for external trends, it's also important to watch for trends in eBooks within our world of libraries. These types of trends are easier to spot because library-centric publications, newsletters, blogs, and periodicals are trying to keep track of the trends for librarians. One of the important trends to watch is eBook pricing. The multiple models, with all of their variations in purchasing and pricing, have not yet stabilized or coalesced. Changes in the models often have a significant impact on budgets and management of the eBook collection. There are currently multiple models which vary by publisher, and there may sometimes even be multiple models used by the same publisher. This is an area of continual change; and, as is talked about throughout the book, libraries will need to manage their budget and services in this environment.

Publisher purchasing and lending models with their varying rules are difficult to manage now, and while it is hoped that this will stabilize as the eBook world matures, some publishers have already decided to go the opposite direction and create even more models. For some titles, publishers are giving libraries multiple options for purchasing an individual title. The same eBook can be purchased with one-year or two-year access, with the price varying by the length of access time purchased. Publishers may start implementing a mix of different models for different types of materials. Travel books might have a one-year expiration, and fiction might have a two-year expiration. Perhaps a publisher will decide that only one of its imprints will have a different model than the other imprints they publish, since it reaches a different audience and may be able to sell at a higher (or lower) rate to libraries. Or publishers may decide that they want to offer multiple options for all of their titles, with each title having multiple ways to purchase it for your library. If the multiple option model proliferates in the library world, it will become increasingly complex for librarians to manage the models used for what was purchased and to determine when it's time to repurchase, since that could vary on a title-by-title basis. Any of these types of changes would need to be incorporated into your spending plan and your collection management plan, and the impact on your library may vary based on what types of materials you tend to purchase.

Self-publishing authors and "vanity" publishing are also an important part of the eBook landscape. Luckily, many of the publications that track what is happening within the publishing market in the United States are devoting time and energy to tracking what is happening in these markets as well. But there are local trends here to watch for too, especially if you have a strong local or regional author or publishing community near you. If there is a thriving self-publishing community in your area, you may have your local authors coming to you and requesting to have eBook copies of their book added to your collection, just as they have done with print versions. They may now provide EPUB versions that they want to donate or have the library purchase. If the content fits within your collection scope, it may be a good addition to your eBook collection, and is something you'd consider purchasing or accepting as a donation.

With print copies of donated materials, you already have a process in place to add titles to your collection that come in this way. However, you may or may not have the ability to add an eBook copy of the title. If you've created your own eBook system, adding a self-published title from a self-published author is likely no different from your process when adding titles from a publisher. But if you have contracted with an eBook vendor, most likely you don't have the ability to add an eBook from a self-published author, or from smaller or local publishers that they don't work with. You may need to give a simplified explanation, based on the information provided in Chapter 2, as to why you don't have the technical means to accept their eBook. And you'll need to be in conversation with your vendor about how to address this type of situation, especially if this is content you'd normally be able to add to your collection in other formats. Vendors may already have processes in place so that you can connect the author to the vendor for consideration. This is another place where there can be, and hopefully will be, more changes coming to this situation. Library eBook vendors may develop ways where you could add a local author's works to the library collection even if the titles are not part of the vendor's offerings. At present, if you have contracted with a vendor for eBooks, you may need a procedure, talking points, or even a policy as to how to handle self-published eBooks, especially if you are receiving frequent requests to add titles and are unable to do so. But the procedure, talking points, or policy will need to be revised as self-publishing and its relation to the library eBook world changes. Watching what is happening in this ever-increasing world of self-publishing will give you time to plan rather than only react, and to have a response that works for your community as this is in flux.

CHANGES IN OTHER FORMATS

What's happening with the fortunes and development in within the audio book formats is obviously tied to our discussion of eBooks, since both formats are working from the same source material. Many library eBook vendors are also offering eAudio products, so what's trending in audio in relation to eBooks is easy to watch. There are several library vendors offering music and video products, and it's good to see what paths library vendors are taking as well as what is happening generally in the commercial world of video and music. What happens in one industry sometimes translates or has repercussion on other industries. For example, if the video/visual and music industries develop new delivery models for content, something different from streaming, for instance, and they are ones that the public embraces, other industries will look to see if they can be adapted for their formats, in our case, eBooks. There may be substantial changes to platforms that have far-reaching technical implications for a library. Most likely there will be a warning if there is seismic change in something like a delivery model, but the timeline for adjusting to changes of this sort continues to get shorter and shorter.

Music and video was used in this example, but if there is a change in the delivery model with any format that you have in your collection, it's good to note what is changing for that format and contemplate how those changes might affect other formats like eBooks.

THE ROLE OF BIG DATA

When you buy a physical book, publishers lose track of it as soon as the purchase is made. They know they sold a copy, and they know how many copies a bookstore or online outlet sold, but they don't know who purchased a specific copy or what that person did with the book after it was purchased. Was it read immediately? Did it sit in a "To Be Read" pile at the purchaser's house for months and was then read in the space of a day? Were the first few chapters read, but then the reader stopped? Was the book ever opened at all? Or was it given to another reader, and what did that new reader do with it?

An eBook is a digital file that companies are keeping track of for a wide range of reasons, from keeping the file from being pirated to keeping track of where you stopped reading on one device so the eBook will open to the same page on a second device. With this format, what someone does with an eBook and how they are interacting with each copy of the book is now known to publishers. Data is now available about how eBooks are read, since all of the details about how a reader uses the book need to be tracked to make the reading experience possible. Publishers now know how many people read an eBook within 24 hours of purchasing. They know how many people gave up on page 10. They know what favorite sentences are highlighted, and what books never get that type of notation from readers.

The collection and analysis of this massive amount of data has the potential to change what types of books are published and how publishers produce eBooks. It's likely that publishers are already using this data to give the market more of the type of books that readers of eBooks are purchasing. The data they have on books that readers buy, download, and read can be used to try out the different types of eBooks that we talked about as publishing trends earlier in this chapter. Using this data to expand offerings or target offerings is one aspect of how big data can be used. It also can be used to stop producing some types of content altogether or produce fewer titles if the data has said that the people may purchase a copy, but then let it sit on their device without being opened. But perhaps publishers will not care whether a title has been read or not as long as there has been a purchase; books that are purchased (or checked out) is still a valid activity, even if a book isn't read immediately or highlighted heavily.

In 2001, the Nielsen Company (http://www.nielsen.com/us/en/about-us.html) launched its book publishing product, BookScan, to capture actual book sales data. Prior to the widespread adoption of the BookScan product by the publishing industry, sales data was held only by individual publishing companies. Now sales data is complied, analyzed, and shared with the publishing industry. Like eBook data, publishers now have big data on physical books as well. Publishers do not have information as specific as to when someone plucked a book off a "To Be Read" pile and actually read it, but they have a lot of information about where and what books are selling, regionally and internationally. While this is a tool for the publishing industry, some data is reported out in news stories. Physical sale data could affect what types of books are published and sold as eBooks. Publishers can use this data to make decisions about what is published in eBook version and what is published in physical version. Those decisions then have an effect on what's in our library collections.

Publishers could also use the data to make editing decisions. Data exists that show where readers skip through parts and where they slow down. The data could be used to find elements that readers tend to skip over. If data analysts can identify elements that readers tend to find less interesting, perhaps publishers will edit out similar parts from an author's manuscript. Authors may embrace and accept this type of editing or they may not. If not, there may be another surge into more self-publishing, for authors and readers who are interested in a different experience.

Not only are publishers collecting big data; if you contract with a library vendor to provide eBooks, the company you are contracting with is collecting big data too. Vendors now have a lot of this same type of data on what your patrons are doing with eBooks. If you have your own platform, you now have big data as well. What librarians should do with big data is a topic for important discussion. As a library professional, librarians are careful about data with regards to what patrons are doing. Librarians believe that patrons have a fundamental right to privacy with regards to what they do with library materials. But now librarians may have big data that allows them to serve patrons better by giving them more of what they want based on data analysis. You need to think about the thresholds as to where you are willing to go with the use of big data and where you are not willing to go. And you need to consider your obligation related to your contracts with vendors about what you would like them to provide and what is beyond what you and other librarians think vendors should collect and store. Big data exists; librarians need to be aware of what corporations are doing with the data or thinking about doing with the data. And you need to determine what your own stance is on the data that you collect and/or have access to.

How the data on the reading of eBooks translates to reading physical books and what publishers will ultimately do with the data in terms of content published is yet to be known. Tracking how the discussions progress with regards to big data and the publishing industry is important. The use of big data could fundamentally change what is being published. Likewise, keeping track of what vendors are collecting about library patrons as well as how they are using that data to shape their business decisions is important to know.

THE CUSTOMER RELATIONSHIP

In the pre-eBook era, publishers were the owners of the content, and the bookseller/bookstore or library was the owner of the customer relationship. But in this eBook era, some publishers are creating a direct connection to consumers by creating websites from which consumers can purchase directly. Publishers selling directly to readers may be a way for publishers to create their own relationship with consumers in response to changes in the marketplace, like the closing of the national chain booksellers and independent bookstores. It may also be a result of having more data about what is selling and where. The holiday reader's advisory hotline mentioned earlier will be giving publishers data through their conversations with customers. They'll have data on what types of books customers are looking to give as gifts, and what type of books customers want more because they want something just like _______. By creating a direct relationship, publishers can capture even more data to make content or marketing decisions. Librarians value a long history of strong patron relationships. As other entities create relationships with library patrons, librarians need to watch what parts of these new relationships are appealing to customers and if possible add those parts to library offerings as well.

Changes in customer relationships are often reported on in publications that track publishing world and the broader bookselling world, since it's an important part of understanding how books connect with readers. The library professional publications also watch for changes in this relationship for the reasons mentioned, especially in an environment where there are so many changes under way. If a publisher adds a new service that creates a strong patron relationship between the customer and the company, librarians should be looking to see if that service can be offered or adapted to the library world in order to maintain and strengthen relationships with patrons. In general, patrons may not know or care which publisher has published books by their favorite authors. However, this could change as publishers are better able to provide eBooks directly to readers through their online sites, and to develop a relationship directly with customer themselves.

LINKED DATA

The term *linked data* refers to the ability of making connections between types or pieces of data that makes it more discoverable on the web. One set of data that hasn't been readily available when doing a web search is data from libraries. Information from OPACs about what titles a library owns has not been readily discoverable on the web. If you search your library's name, your website will pop up. But if one of your patrons is searching for a book, your library would not show up in the search results as an option for obtaining the title. Using linked data would allow a library to tell potential patrons who are searching for a title, including an eBook version of a title, that their nearest library or library system might be an option. Employing linked data to get library information onto the web opens a whole new world of possibilities and there are companies, including ILS vendors, creating and exploring ways to best gather library data and make it available for Internet search results. If information about library collections is readily discoverable when doing a web search, it puts any library into the consciousness of people every time they do a search and relevant library information appears in the search results. There is tremendous potential to use linked data and help libraries answer with a resounding "yes!" to that recurring question about relevant services. Using linked data for library information just is beginning, but the words *linked data* are ones to watch for when your ILS vendor is telling you about new developments it is working on, or just when you see those words in the media. Using linked data has the possibility to be revolutionary for libraries, especially when a patron is searching online, without first going to the library website, and can discover an eBook copy of a book that the library owns and he or she can then check out and access within moments on his or her phone.

RESEARCH ON READING HABITS

With the advent of the eBook marketplace, there has been renewed interest in the reading habits and preferences of the general public. The PEW Research Center (http://www.pewresearch.org) has undertaken a number of research projects seeking to understand trends in reading and the way the reading public engages with books, including eBooks. PEW has also spent considerable time researching and surveying what the general public opinion is on a wide variety of library-related topics, as well as trends in Internet and online use and device preferences.

Numerous other companies or groups with a particular focus have a new or renewed interest in what, how, how much, and where people are reading. Some groups have a long history of surveying readers and, with the adoption of the eBook, have simply added that into the mix of data collected. The Romance Writers of America (RWA, https://www.rwa.org) has regularly surveyed readers, and publishes its findings on its website about who is buying and reading romance. While its focus is primarily on romance publishing and romance readers, its findings are often of interest to the general publishing and author communities also.

Chapter 1 covered discovering what your patrons want in terms of content in an eBook collection. There are numerous groups and organizations that are devoted to readers and authors of many types of fiction and nonfiction for readers of all ages, and the development and use of social media tools allows readers of like types of books to find each other. While it may be impossible for your library to track all of the larger groups like RWA as well as the many smaller groups to discover how their readers' preferences are shifting, it's still important to be aware that the information may be available to you should you need it. If you find your circulation of a type of book is shifting, seeking out these groups may help you discover if there is a bigger overall shift happening, like from physical to eBook, or perhaps back again.

As mobile devices move into classrooms, there are many in the fields of psychology, human development, and many other areas who are interested in all the same questions as groups like RWA. What, how, how much, and where are children and teens reading? The results of some of the academic and semi-academic studies are sometimes picked up and published in the mainstream and library media. If your eBook collection is built as a support for local school curriculum, or if you're planning for your collection to support recreational reading for children and teens, watching for trends in how children are reading books will help you purchase accordingly. Likewise, there may be trends about certain age groups preferring physical over the eBook version for certain types of reading. Because the eBook has become ubiquitous only recently, it is important to continually watch for new research and studies being released, especially as the studies are reported in local and national media. This information is of course useful to tailor your collections to match what your patrons want, but do check in with the data you have to see if what the studies are reporting matches with what you're seeing in the use of your collection.

How important is it to change quickly in response to a new study? In general, it's best to look at the data you have on the use of your library's eBook collection and see if it matches what you're reading in other places. If it does and it's a significant change, like a double-digit drop in circulation of a type of book, then it may be good to make a change immediately. If not, then perhaps it's something to watch to see if there is switch coming in use and when you see it you can respond accordingly.

CHANGING TECHNOLOGY

Technology changes, shifts, and develops with increasing speed. While the technology in place now works to offer eBooks to library patrons, the technology equation could shift at a moment's notice. What if publishers abandoned the DRM models currently in place in favor of different method entirely? Or what if there was a game-changer, like the public's quick acceptance of using their cell phones to read an eBook, and libraries have a whole new device to support? What if someone invents a new file format that incorporates DRM? Or what if two of the components discussed in Chapter 2 would merge functionality and become one component?

Library vendors track technology changes and developments. In fact, they're constantly working on changing and developing the technical parts that they manage to provide a better patron experience. They are trying to create a better service for patrons than their competitors can offer and that competition is good for libraries. If you are working with library eBook vendors (and even if you're not), it's good to read through their product announcements, especially if they have release notes about technical upgrades and related information. Vendors most likely have more resources to track what the public is doing in the general marketplace than you have time to do. Keeping watch on where the library vendors are putting their time, energy, and money into developing products and services gives you an important insight into what the vendors are thinking is where the overall marketplace is heading next.

LIBRARY ACTIVITY ON REGIONAL, STATE, AND NATIONAL LEVELS

Another trend to note, and another one that's easier for you to follow, is what is happening on regional, state, and national levels. This can be easier to track because it is reported on by the library media. Often there is reporting at the beginning of the project and the end of a project or initiative. Groups of libraries are partnering as consortia to figure out what would be the best practices for purchasing and offering eBooks to their patrons. Consortia in different states are looking at these same issues, although they're not all making the same decisions or trying to achieve the exact same goals. If you read about one of these consortial models in the media and the model intrigues you, keep track of which organization is working on it, the name of the project, and the lead people involved. Their project may or may not show up in the media on a regular basis, but if you are wondering how their project is progressing, they may have built a website or have a staff member that you can contact, and you can follow up with them for an update and see what is happening.

With the creation of Digital Public Library of America (DPLA, http://dp.la) in 2010 we now have a national digital library. DPLA seeks to provide access to not only eBooks but also to other digital objects like photographic images, documents, and audiovisual materials. Your library or your system, if you belong to one, may even be a partner of DPLA. Since DPLA is working on many fronts, including eBooks, digitized images, and other online materials, you may not be aware of all of the projects that are currently under way. Checking out the initiatives listed on its project page is a glimpse into what is of interest on the national level, and may provide you with ideas about ways to connect your patrons to the eBooks and other materials becoming available there.

Other local digital repositories may exist as well. Many states have initiatives for providing increased access to digitized historical materials. Some of the digital objects collected into a state collection could be digital objects from a variety of libraries, both public and academic, as well as historical societies and other entities that have a history of collecting materials. These types of initiatives are sometimes forgotten as eBook collections because there is a broad focus to digitize all types of materials, including photographs, written correspondence, newspapers, audio, and video, as well as books. Because these initiatives are often full of content not found anywhere else, they can have a tremendous interest to your community. But as mentioned, because the collections are filled with objects beyond books, it's easy to forget them or keep them separate as a source of eBook content for your patrons. But since there are usually at least some eBooks available in these collections, it's important to keep them in mind as you plan for your offerings for your patrons.

CHANGES IN THE LAW

As has been mentioned several times throughout the course of this book, the current U.S. copyright law has had an impact on how libraries are able to offer eBooks. While this book is focused on a discussion of providing access to the books themselves, there is a much broader discussion regarding other copyrighted materials that now have a digital component that hadn't been imagined when the law was enacted. Just as it's important to be watching what is developing in the music and video industries in terms of content, delivery mechanisms, devices, and the like, keeping track of the conversation around what the authors and other content creators, as well as publishers and other delivery platforms, would like to see in terms of changes to U.S. and international copyright is also important. There is a natural and expected tension between the makers and producers of content and libraries who wish to make the content as accessible as possible. The producers of content want to profit from, or at least be compensated for, the making and delivery of the content. While libraries purchase content as well, once libraries have the content, they want to be able to continue to provide it to patrons to use for free. Digitized content like eBooks adds a new dimension to this conversation for all parties.

As eBooks have expanded into the market, there has been much discussion of the possible loss of sales for publishers due to libraries offering eBooks. This discussion has led to a surge of research into what value libraries add to the publishing world. *Library Journal* has sponsored research on the topic, as has PEW. Lawmakers are beginning to look at the issues surrounding what it would take to revise copyright law to align the rights around digital objects to what's already in place for physical materials. This would include what the purchaser of digital content is allowed to do with the content once he or she has it, and would affect both the general consumer and libraries. Libraries will want to retain the right to lend any type of material. Producers will want to be sure that they are compensated for material and have controls in place so they don't lose compensation. Consumers will have expectations as to what they can do with material once they've purchased it. There are also overarching philosophical questions to be thought through in terms of how, when, and at what cost content is available. The needs and interests of the multiple parties to this conversation don't necessarily align with one another, at least at first glance. When lawmakers are ready to take on a revision of the U.S. copyright law, there will be many viewpoints coming to the table, and it will be important that librarians watch the trajectory of the discussion.

Related to possible changes in copyright law are the discussions, mostly within the realm of academia at this time, centered on how research is being made available to others in the field. With all of the new methods of sharing in an online world, there are now tensions similar to the copyright discussions in the general marketplace. Many researchers want information widely and easily disseminated in order to collaborate more freely.

Publishers want to maintain controls so that there is not a loss of compensation. It's worth watching both debates, because what is decided in one arena may influence what is decided in the other, and may impact what types of access libraries will be able to provide.

STAYING CONNECTED

From copyright to publishing to big data and linked data, as well as all of the topics you have thought of but are not covered here, there are lots of areas to monitor as you move into providing an eBook collection to your patrons. As you evaluate what issues are most important for you and your community, you'll have to figure out how you want to stay connected to the issues that are most relevant for your needs.

Some of the most obvious places to start are, of course, the library-focused media outlets. Publications like *Library Journal, School Library Journal, American Libraries*, and others are all trying to keep us up to date with developments in the world of eBooks, both in their print publications and through articles that may appear only in their online publications. Because eBooks are still relatively new in the public consciousness, issues and topics related to eBooks are still being reported on in national media, including *USA Today*, the *New York Times*, and the *Washington Post*. There may also be media coverage in local and regional media, and through major online and broadcast news outlets.

Of course, the main way of tracking what is written regarding eBooks is what's published online. Not only are the newspapers represented and searchable on the web, but related social media outlets for them are there as well. Some of the ancillary blogs are a wealth of information if you discover certain papers or reporters who have a strong interest in any of the topics we've talked about from publishing to big data.

Many of the industries talked about in this chapter have conferences dedicated to their products. BookExpo America, the London Book Fair, and the Frankfurt Book Fair are all examples of conferences or fairs dedicated to what is happening in the book world. If you can attend any of these in person, there will be a plethora of information you can gather about what is currently happening in the publishing world and specifically within eBooks. But there are conferences, fairs, and other get-togethers devoted all of the topics talked about in this chapter. Even though your staff may never attend any of these because of travel costs or geographic location, they are worth watching for what is being discussed and presented during these conferences.

Social media is wonderful for monitoring what is happening at and during these shows. For example, the International Consumer Electronics Show (CES, http://cesweb .org) is not open to the general public, but many professionals and members of the media who attend do blog or write longer pieces about what is covered at this influential trade show. The CES is where new devices are launched and modeled. What is presented or launched at CES may be the next device you will see in the hands of your patrons in a few months. When you discover conferences and trade shows that are of particular interest to you and you think what's happening at the conference will affect your patrons, search for their conference information. Then look for the leaders in their fields, find their social media presence, and follow their conversation.

Another example of an industry-specific convention is the Toy Fair, which is an annual trade show for businesses specializing in toys and entertainment products for children. In the toy world, books are classed as entertainment products and toy stores often carry a selection of books as part of their overall inventory. Among the exhibitors at the annual Toy Fair are major U.S. publishing houses, so publishers are obviously finding these types of tangential conventions valuable. A toy vendor may not find a new way to get books in the hands of children, but then again, it might. Following what trade shows and conventions publishers are putting in resources to attend gives us insight into where else books and eBooks might be sold or different ways in which book content is delivered to consumers. Again, social media is a good way to follow product launches and discussions about changes in industries where books don't play a big part, but what develops within that industry may have an impact on the book industry later.

Library conferences can be great sources of information as well, since the library community is also trying to monitor the issues that affect the library world on key issues like eBooks access. State, regional, and national conferences can all provide insights into what other library professionals are thinking, doing, trying, or advocating with regards to eBooks in libraries. Again, even if you can't attend these conferences in person, there are multiple ways to keep track of the conversation via online tools.

Blogs and newsletters abound as well, and there are many book-centered ones like Shelf Awareness (http://www.shelf-awareness.com) to ones produced by individual publishers. Just as there are blogs and newsletters for every type of reader, there are blogs and newsletters for topics in copyright, topics related to big data, as well as many of the related topics covered in this chapter.

Once you have located the sources or the conversations to follow, you need to figure out what to keep track of on a regular basis. Of course, it is impossible to follow everything that is happening that has any possible relation to the world of eBooks. Prioritize what is most important for you, what you are most interested in, or what concerns your library the most, and try to divide the work so it doesn't all fall to one person on your staff to monitor all of the areas or publications. Share the monitoring of related topics and figure out a way to regularly swap information you've gleaned. Then determine when it makes sense to share things you see on the horizon with your stakeholders, when you need to ask questions of vendors, when you need to prepare new plans to accommodate changes, and even when you might want to join a conversation on a national level.

CONCLUSION

The physical material in our libraries may seldom be of any interest to anyone outside of our library staff and patrons and local community. Once it has been purchased, librarians are the only ones who know the "story" of the material. They are the only ones who know how much the material has circulated, who know something about who has used the material even though the commitment to patron privacy means the information is not usually kept. While publishers and others would be interested in what happens with the library's physical materials, this is a story that libraries own. In contrast, the story about how eBooks are used in individual libraries is not one that librarians own alone. The eBooks that libraries are purchasing are of great interest to numerous parties, from publishers to library vendors. Because of their online nature, not only do libraries have the data about how eBooks are being used but so do the publishers and vendors. This sharing of the eBook story means that librarians also need to track the developments in related professions and topics looking for what may impact eBooks in libraries.

It's impossible to predict everything that might impact librarians in terms of how libraries offer eBooks. It's also impossible to be watching all related topics and reading every related blog or newspaper report. But if you can, divide the monitoring between other people even using perhaps nontraditional sources. For example, you may have board members who work in a technology field and they can let you know when they hear something about linked data that might be interesting to explore in the library world. Or your library may have a volunteer who works in retail and has heard of a new way that publishers are marketing eBooks that might be possible for your library to consider providing also. This connection to a broader world allows you to be proactive and talk about what you do as having increased relevance not only to your dedicated patrons, but as part of society in general.

CHAPTER 9

Conclusion

If there's one thing to expect as you build and manage your eBook collection, it's change. There will continue to be new formats, new platforms, new ways to connect books and readers; once you get started, you'll need to continue to explore new options, and remain aware of changes and trends happening in the broader publishing and technology environments.

Even as this book is written, there are new ways to connect books and readers being developed, and new strategies to support both the technical and service requirements needed to ensure that books can get into the hands (or devices) of the people who want to read them. As you are developing, or expanding, your collections and services, you'll want to stay in tune with what's happening for your readers, as well as trends in the publishing and device industries. What worked when you got started with eBooks may not be where you want to stay as your community changes, or as the broader industry changes. Staying connected by following trends in publishing and technology, and by soliciting ongoing, meaningful feedback from your patrons, you should be able to navigate the changes happening in this area.

We hope this book has helped you prepare for what lies ahead. These are exciting and challenging times for libraries, and there will continue to be changes in the eBook world that provide us with opportunities to rethink the way we select out collections and get books, in all formats, in the hands (or devices) of readers in our communities.

INDEX

ABOUT THE AUTHORS

MICHELE MCGRAW and GAIL MUELLER SCHULTZ both have over twenty years' experience in public libraries in a variety of roles. They currently work for Hennepin County Library in Minnesota. Michele is HCL's Information Services Manager, working with staff providing Information and Readers Advisory services, and she also works with the website and other online content. Gail is the Manager of Collection and Technical Services, and she also oversees the Library's Special Collections, Digitization and Preservation Department. Michele and Gail are constantly working in collaboration with each other and their colleagues to bring the best collections and services possible to Hennepin County patrons.